Ben Nevis

The unlikely story of a
great steeplechase horse

by
Anne Conyngham Baetjer Jenkins

Grateful acknowledgement is made to
The National Steeplechase Foundation
for their support.

Foreword

This book was begun in 1988. I feel fortunate that I was able to interview, at that time, almost all of the people central to this story.

I was lucky to have Dale Austin read and comment on an early version and to have had Peter Winants give me advice and put his files at my disposal. Tim Forster, Wallace Lanahan, Hugh O'Donovan, and Pattie Penniman were kind to answer my questions. I am sorry that they did not get to see the finished project, and particularly sorry that I did not start this book in time to interview my uncle, Redmond Conyngham Stewart Jr., before his death in 1986. Margaret Worrall's books and advice were particularly helpful. My thanks to the following people who spent time answering my questions and/or who lent me photos and archival material.

Michael Bannister	Grace MacMillan
Jeep Cochran	Turney McKnight
Lee McShane Cox	Irv Naylor
Nancy Dougherty	Tim Naylor
Bruce Fenwick	Paddy Neilson
Charlie Fenwick III	Richard Pitman
Redmond Finney	Anita Prentice
Beth Fenwick Garner	Nat Prentice
Rita Goolsby	Barrie B. Reightler
Jay Griswold	Johnny Shaw
Kathy Ingalls	Nina Strawbridge
Douglas Lees	Graham Thorner
Cappy Jackson	Minnie Watriss

My greatest thanks go to Charlie Fenwick and Ann Stewart. They spent many hours answering my questions and spilling out for me their memories of Ben Nevis. I finished an initial manuscript in 1989, and then put the project aside for 20 years. When I began to rewrite the book in the fall of 2009, I had more questions which they answered patiently. I am very grateful; the book could not have been written without their help.

Annie Jenkins
Welshes Cradle
January 2010

Strawberry Roan

I was hangin' 'round town, just spendin' my time
Out of a job, not earnin' a dime
A feller steps up and he said, "I suppose
You're a bronc fighter from looks of your clothes."
"You figures me right, I'm a good one," I claim
"Do you happen to have any bad ones to tame?"
Said "He's got one, a bad one to buck
At throwin' good riders, he's had lots of luck."

I gets all het up and I ask what he pays
To ride this old nag for a couple of days
He offered me ten; I said, "I'm your man,
A bronc never lived that I couldn't span."
He said: "Get your saddle, I'll give you a chance."
In his buckboard we hopped and he drives to the ranch
I stayed 'til mornin' and right after chuck
I stepped out to see if this outlaw can buck.

Down in the horse corral standin' alone
Is an old Caballo, a Strawberry Roan
His legs are all spavined, he's got pigeon toes
Little pig eyes and a big Roman nose
Little pin ears that touched at the tip
A big 44 brand was on his left hip
U-necked and old, with a long, lower jaw
I could see with one eye, he's a regular outlaw.

5

I gets the blinds on 'im and it sure is a fright
Next comes the saddle and I screws it down tight
Then I steps on 'im and I raises the blinds
Get outta the way boys, he's gonna unwind
He sure is a frog-walker, he heaves a big sigh
He only lacks wings, for to be on the fly
He turns his old belly right up to the sun
He sure is a sun-fishin', son-of-a-gun.

He's about the worst bucker I've seen on the range
He'll turn on a Nickel and give you some change
He hits on all fours and goes up on high
Leaves me a spinnin' up there in the sky
I turns over twice and I comes back to earth
I lights in a cussin' the day of his birth
I know there are ponies that I cannot ride
There's some of them left, they haven't all died.
I'll bet all my money, the man ain't alive
That'll stay with Old Strawberry
When he makes his high dive.

Marty Robbins

Introduction

The story of the horse Ben Nevis – his purchase, his training, and his racing career – has an improbable beginning and an unlikely ending. The beginning came when Redmond Conyngham Stewart Jr., an American from Baltimore, decided to buy the gelding, sight unseen and with a reputation for being difficult, over the dinner table during a grouse-shooting trip in Yorkshire, England, during the summer of 1974.

Ben Nevis was brought to America and given to Stewart's son-in-law, Charles C. "Charlie" Fenwick Jr., to train and ride. After months of patient handling, and to the astonishment of all concerned, Ben Nevis proved to be a fast and faultless jumper. With Charlie on his back and Stewart's support, Ben Nevis won all 12 of the timber races in which he was entered over the succeeding four years. Two of his wins were in the Maryland Hunt Cup, a race generally acknowledged as the most challenging in the steeplechase world.

Redmond Stewart and Charlie then decided to send Ben Nevis back to England to train for the English Grand National, the most highly regarded and elusive prize in steeplechase racing. Charlie moved with his wife, Ann – Stewart's daughter – and their children to the United Kingdom to train and ride Ben Nevis. After eight months of preparation, Ben Nevis fell in a collision at the 15th fence of the Grand National. Against the prevailing opinion, Charlie, Ann, and Redmond Stewart decided to leave the horse in

England for the following year in order to have another try in the Grand National.

On March 29, 1980, Ben Nevis again lined up at the start. What followed proved Ben Nevis worthy of the faith that Redmond Stewart and the Fenwicks had in their horse, and proved Ben Nevis worthy of the following words borrowed from horseman, Edwin Anthony.

> Every horse race has a winner; that's a fact. And just because a horse wins an otherwise important race, that does not make that horse particularly special, other than it may have been the best (that day) of an average field of Thoroughbreds. Greatness must be earned – gauged against the clock, measured against the history books. There must be dominance and consistency, across state borders and time zones, over varying track conditions, and against the best competition available. When these conditions are met, then a discussion of history and greatness can begin.

Chapter One

The morning of Saturday, March 29, 1980, dawns clear in Aintree, England. It is race day in Britain. All over the country, people have made their bets on the Grand National. A large percentage of the British population bets on only one event a year, and that event is the Grand National at Aintree. Just as most Europeans can name the teams in the World Cup, and most Americans can name the teams playing in the Super Bowl, most Britons know the top horses racing in the National. Newspapers and television programs have been full of analysis for weeks. The names of the favored horses – Delmoss, Jer, Rough and Tumble, Royal Stuart, Rubstic, The Pilgaric, and Zongalero – have been heard in the pubs and discussed in kitchens and drawing rooms from the top of Scotland to the bottom of Cornwall. The jockeys and trainers and owners have been interviewed, and their records, as well as their private lives, are fodder for the press.

The crowd of race goers is beginning to gather at the famous venue. There will be around 68,000 of them by post time for the Grand National, and an estimated 600,000 people around the world will be watching on television. Thirty horses will line up at the start. Their jockeys hope to get them over 30 fences on a four-and-a-half mile course that ends with a 494-yard run-in to the finish. Tragically, horses have lost their lives in the race during its 138 previous runnings. This year will be particularly challenging because the race course is sodden. There was torrential rain yesterday, and the ground is described as a "gluepot." The horses will grow tired pulling their hooves out of the mud, and sinking into the ground will mean that each jump will be that much higher.

One American-owned horse will line up at the start this afternoon, a horse that has attracted little recent attention from the press. His name is Ben Nevis and although he is named for the highest mountain in the British Isles, he is small, a chestnut standing about 16 hands. He is neither powerful looking nor exceptionally well proportioned. In fact, his trainer, Tim Forster, has described him as "weedy looking." But Ben Nevis has won the Maryland Hunt Cup twice and Forster knows that any horse that can win the Maryland Hunt Cup is worthy of respect. Ben Nevis not only inspires respect, but also affection in those who have worked with him.

"He has a chance because he can jump and he is such a brave horse who stays forever," says Forster. Ben Nevis's jockey, Charlie Fenwick, adds, "You could sleep in his stall, and he wouldn't hurt you. He is very kind. And you can't help but love a horse that tries so hard."

Ben Nevis was trying hard one year earlier when he and Charlie got to the 15th fence of the Grand National. The 15th fence, known as the Chair, is the biggest on the course: five feet, two inches high, three feet wide, and with a five foot ditch in front of it. Two horses that had lost their riders were running parallel in front of the Chair when Ben Nevis and Charlie arrived at the fence. Although horse and rider tried to avoid the melee, there were too many oncoming horses to avert a collision. As a result, Ben Nevis fell along with eight other horses. A guard at the fence said that

Ben Nevis tried to jump a horse, the ditch, and the fence, but he couldn't clear all three.

Today, Ben Nevis will get another chance, although the bookies are not giving him much of one, listing him at 40-1 odds. Last year was different; the press and the pundits had been very interested in him. They had not forgotten Jay Trump, the only American-owned and American-ridden horse to win the Grand National. That was in 1965. Jay Trump also had won the Maryland Hunt Cup, and the British understand that almost any Hunt Cup winner has the potential to win at Aintree.

Leading up to last year's race, there had been many articles in the papers and sporting journals about Ben Nevis, his owner Redmond Stewart, and jockey Charlie Fenwick. Charlie's grit and perseverance riding as an amateur against British professionals were mentioned approvingly. Stewart was lauded for the sporting gesture of bringing horse and rider to the U.K. to live and train for eight months. However, Ben Nevis has not won a race in Britain since being brought over from the U.S. and with his fall in last year's National, interest in him has all but dried up.

That suits Forster fine. Last year, he felt that there was too much pressure on his stable, on the horse, and on the rider as a result of press attention and the many Americans who came over to see Ben Nevis and Charlie in the race. "It all became a distraction to the business at hand," Forster says. He prefers this year's lower profile.

Some of those Americans describe Forster as the stereotypic Englishman: reserved, formal, and traditional. Educated at Eton and having served with Britain's 11th Hussars regiment, he is known respectfully as "The Captain." Although he can be charm-

ing, he does not suffer fools gladly, and he is very clear when someone runs afoul of his expectations. It is to Charlie's great credit that
he has won Forster's respect.

"At first I had more doubts about Charlie than the horse,
because I didn't know Charlie well enough then to know how determined he is," Forster explains. "He has adapted himself to the
different conditions over here, and he is highly intelligent and as
fit as a human being could be."

Forster has won the Grand National once before, in 1972,
with a horse named Well To Do. That win and many others over
the past 18 years have earned Forster a reputation as a successful
trainer. He also has gained a name for being pessimistic. And on
this March day in 1980, he is living up to that reputation; far from
thinking Ben Nevis might win, he just hopes that the horse can get
around the course.

Charlie Fenwick will ride Ben Nevis again today. Although
Charlie is an amateur in a professional's world here in the U.K., he
is as tough as any pro. Ben Nevis was an extremely difficult horse
when Charlie first began to work with him, and it is due almost
solely to him that the horse became manageable enough to ride in
races. Someone with less resolve and stubbornness would not have
persevered with the horse.

Charlie's grandfather, Howard Bruce, owned Billy Barton,
the horse that finished second in the 1928 English Grand National. From childhood on, Charlie has heard stories about the great
English race, and he grew up with a map of the Aintree course on
his bedroom wall.

Charlie learned to ride when he was seven, riding in his first
race 10 years later. That was the same year Tommy Smith won the

English Grand National on Jay Trump. Charlie's uncle had trained Jay Trump, and Charlie knew Tommy from working around his uncle's stable.

"It was really Tommy's success that put the idea in my head and my brother Bruce's head that we might ride in the Grand National," Charlie says. "Because Tommy Smith did it – and he did it with Bobby Fenwick as trainer – we thought we could do it. That was our attitude."

Although Charlie was an experienced rider when he arrived here in England 20 months ago, competing against professional jockeys has been a difficult and humbling experience. Both Charlie and Ben Nevis have been challenged to adjust to the conditions of British racing.

After last year's attempt at the National, it was not possible for Charlie and Ann to stay in England for another year. Therefore, Charlie has commuted from Baltimore, Maryland, to ride in races here over the past year. He and Ann flew over on Thursday, two days ago, and yesterday he rode out at Forster's yard. He was dismayed by how tired he felt. He is fighting jet leg on a day when he has his second and, most likely, his last chance to ride in a race he has been dreaming about for most of his life.

This will be Charlie's 17th race in the British Isles over the past 17 months. He arrived full of confidence, some might say cocky. This morning he is older and wiser, and with experience has come humility. He is feeling, as he says, "a heightened anxiety," but he is ready for the race to begin.

The owners of the horses, with their entourages, have begun to make their way up to their boxes. Unfortunately, Ben Nevis's

English Grand National on March 27, 1931
Jumping Becher's Brook on the first circuit

owner is not here. Redmond Stewart Jr. is back in the U.S. with his wife, who is ill.

Stewart grew up foxhunting, race-riding, and hearing stories of the English Grand National. In the 1920s and 1930s, his parents subscribed to a service that supplied photos taken at the race's big fences. Those photos were carefully preserved in scrapbooks and, one can imagine, examined over and over by the family.

"The whole of foxhunting America would rather win your Grand National than any other race," Stewart has admitted to a British journalist.

Stewart is a man of contrasts. He approaches life with an exuberance and unconventionality that can be extremely charming.

He is, by turns, highly entertaining, argumentative, generous, and unpredictable. Even his less extreme behavior might be described as eccentric. He once was playing in a golf tournament at a prestigious club in Rhode Island when his ball landed in a shallow area of a small pond. Stewart proceeded to take off his shoes, socks, and trousers, wade into the water, and hit the ball out. He won the tournament.

Stewart was in the stands at Aintree to watch Jay Trump's victory and he traveled from Baltimore last year to cheer on Charlie and Ben Nevis. Today he is in Florida with his wife and two of their daughters. American television does not broadcast the Grand National, so they have arranged for an English friend to put a telephone call through to them just before the start of the race. Their friend will hold the phone up to the television so that they can hear the race announcer's voice. It is just after 3:00 p.m. in the UK, nearly post time, and the Stewarts are waiting for the call.

Chapter Two

This story begins in the summer of 1974, when Redmond and Ann Stewart of Glyndon, Maryland, went to Yorkshire on a shooting trip with a group of their friends. The Stewarts regularly visited the British Isles to shoot and to foxhunt.

The shooting party included Bobby and Minnie Fenwick, Spencer Janney, James McHenry, William and Grace MacMillan, and Nicholas and Pattie Penniman, all old friends from Maryland. One of the moors where they shot, Wuthering Heights, belonged to an Englishman, Michael Bannister, of Coniston Hall. An engaging and hospitable man, Bannister invited the whole group to dinner on the night before the party was to split up. Late in the evening the conversation turned to horses. Stewart allowed as how he was looking for a horse, which was apparently news to his wife. Bannister, leaning back in his chair and looking down the long table lit by candlelight, said he knew of a horse named Ben Nevis that might be available.

"I've heard he's a bit of a mad one, a little wild, but he may have talent," Bannister said.

Stewart peered at him through the cigar smoke over his glass of port. "Oh, he probably just needs a good rider. I'm sure my son-in-law could ride him," he said.

"Well, I know my friend Billy Hope broke this horse," Bannister responded. "Billy is a livery man and he is an artist at breaking horses. And he says Ben Nevis is too much for the girl who has him."

A lively discussion ensued with the rest of the guests, all of them knowledgeable, at least in their own minds, about horses, arguing the pros and cons of taking on a horse known to be difficult. Stewart smelled a challenge and reiterated that a good jockey would be able to solve the horse's problems.

Later, Bannister remembered, "It was getting late and finally Redmond Stewart stood up and said, 'Heck, I'll buy the damn horse, and Charlie will ride him.'"

The party broke up, and the Americans went back to their hotel.

The next morning Ben Nevis's owner was contacted and in the light of day but not admitting to any second thoughts, Stewart saw the sense in asking Bobby Fenwick to take a look at the horse for him. Fenwick was an outstanding horseman, and Stewart respected his opinion. He asked Fenwick to confirm that the horse at least was put together tolerably and had no obvious injuries. Stewart did not go himself because, according to Hugh O'Donovan, a close friend of Stewart's who was in England at the time, "He said the heck with it; he didn't want to get up that early."

Fenwick's wife, Minnie Watriss, recalls, "Bobby and I had already packed and were dressed to leave when we got a call arranging to see the horse. It was literally at the 11th hour and it was pouring with rain. We had to dig out the rubber boots which, of course, were at the bottom of the duffle bag. Bobby put them on with his gray traveling suit, and a farmhand came and picked him up to go see the horse."

Fenwick was taken out to the small farm where Ben Nevis was turned out in a paddock. The light was bad, and no one was there to show the horse. Fenwick couldn't even make out the horse very well, much less judge how he moved. Finally, he did the only thing he could think of – he picked up a rock and threw it in the horse's general direction to make him run. Run, Ben Nevis duly did, and he seemed to move well.

Back at the hotel later, Fenwick reported to Stewart that as far as he could see, the horse was well made, looked athletic, and there was nothing obviously wrong with him. With that, an offer was made, accepted, and the deal was done. For $6,900, Stewart purchased a horse he had never seen, with mediocre breeding and a reputation for being difficult to ride. Had Stewart cared to look him up in the most recent *Hunter Chasers and Point-to-pointers*, he would have read Ben Nevis's prospects described as follows: "May turn out like his half-brother – speedy, a bad jumper, and only able to last a bare three miles."

Robert Wilson was the English farmer who owned Ben Nevis. Wilson had acquired the horse from Pattenden's Exceat Stud Farm in East Sussex when Ben Nevis failed to reach his reserve at the Newmarket sales. At that time, he was a 4-year-old gelding, unbroken and unhandled. His sire was a little-known stallion called Casmiri, winner of seven races from six to 12 furlongs, whose career ended in 1959 after once unseating his rider, the next time being pulled up, and the third time refusing. He was given away and went to stud for a fee of 50 pounds, 8 shillings.

Ben Nevis's dam, Ben Trumiss, was the broodmare at Patten-den's. Her racing career consisted of running three times unplaced on the flat as a 2-year-old, and her other foals were of no account.

Wilson took Ben Nevis to Billy Hope, a local trainer with a few horses, who broke Ben Nevis. When the horse came back to Wilson's farm, Jane Porter, Wilson's daughter, began to ride him. She entered him in three point-to-points, one at a ladies open at the Cheshire forest, which he won. He fell in both of the other races and did not finish. The local talk that got back to Bannister was that Porter just wasn't strong enough to control him.

According to British newspaper accounts after Ben Nevis had become famous, Jane Porter had had a bad fall just before Stewart inquired about buying the horse. In addition, the family had been feeling that they had too many horses to cope with at that time. Although Stewart's offer came out of the blue, the circumstances added up to a willingness to sell Ben Nevis. However, when inter-viewed after the 1980 Grand National, Wilson stated that they had been "very loathe to part with him."

When the Stewarts arrived home in Maryland, they began to make arrangements to ship Ben Nevis to the U.S.

Chapter Three

There were reasons other than whim that Redmond Stewart bought Ben Nevis. He had owned horses and hunted and raced them for most of his life. It was said that in the opinion of Baltimore County foxhunters, Stewart was the rare example of a man who could afford to carry on the traditions of a sport and did his best to accomplish that mission. He was always interested in horses and riders and hounds. He could be irascible at times, but he was kind and fun, and he was a sportsman in the truest sense of the word. He loved a challenge and relished competition. In those traits he was a true son of his parents and grandparents.

Stewart's father, Redmond Conyngham Stewart, was born in 1873. He was one of 14 children of Charles Morton Stewart who owned a fleet of sailing vessels engaged in the coffee trade between Baltimore and Rio de Janeiro. The family lived in Green Spring Valley, and horses and dogs were part of the fabric of their lives. A letter written by Redmond Sr. to his friend John B. Hannum reads, "I often went night-hunting when a small boy, and well remember when I was eight or nine years old getting back home between three and four o'clock in the morning on my little pony."

Redmond Sr. began working with hounds when he was about 13 years old, and when he was 18, he and his younger brother, Plunkett, became two of the founders of the Green Spring Valley Hounds; that same year Redmond Sr. began his 25-year tenure as master and huntsman. He also participated in the first running of the Maryland Hunt Cup. In his words, "When this race was start-ed, way back in 1894, the whole idea was to have pleasant rivalry between the Elkridge and the Green Spring Valley Hunt Clubs and at the end of the season to have this contest largely to find out who had the best hunters. From the beginning, we have kept this in mind. In the first race, my brother-in-law, John McHenry, beat me by a neck on a stout half-bred named 'Johnny Miller.'" (That John McHenry's son, James McHenry, was the one with Redmond Stewart Jr. on the night Ben Nevis was purchased 80 years later.)

Redmond Sr. went on to ride an amazing 14 more times in the Maryland Hunt Cup; he won it in 1904 on his beloved hunter Landslide, finished second five times, and took third four times. He also arranged and was the first winner of a moonlight steeple-chase in 1897, a one and three-quarter mile race over seven white-washed board fences that were jumped by the light of a harvest moon. Participants were required to wear nightclothes over their riding clothes.

The moonlight steeplechase wasn't run every year and had not been run at all for 20 years when Redmond Sr. decided to revive it in 1930. His son, Redmond Jr., was 24 years old that year. Redmond Sr. sent invitations to the original participants: "This close organization should go down from the original nine to nine others by appointment by original members. . . no race should be postponed because of clouds over the moon, except by unanimous consent."

Additionally, he wrote his nephew Frank A. "Downey" Bon-sal, "It seems to me that if we could have but one circle of the Maryland Hunt Cup course on the Worthington Valley side, not over the same panels as the big race, but in the same fences, whitewashing the fences and boards, making four panels, and cutting off the tops of the inside posts, we would have a lovely course."

The race was run, with results as follows:

1. Holmes Alexander, member in place of W. Irvine Cross on Alexander B. Griswold's horse;
2. Redmond Stewart Jr., appointee of Frank B. Smith on his mother's (Katharine Stewart) horse;
3. James McHenry, member in place of Jervis Spencer on his own horse;
4. Redmond Stewart Sr. on his own horse.

The other participants were Thomas Cover, appointee of James Piper; George Blakiston, appointee of Jack Ewing; Reimen McIntosh, appointee of Frank A. Bonsal Jr.; Daniel Baugh Brewster, member in place of Arthur B. Hall; and George Brown Jr. Many of the descendants of these men are active in Maryland's steeplechase community to this day.

The foxhunting communities in the mid-Atlantic region also date back to before the turn of the last century, and are also derived from many of these same families. When Redmond Sr.'s sister Ellinor married Frank A. Bonsal Sr., Redmond gave them 15 couples of hounds, and Bonsal established the Harford Hunt. Plunkett Stewart moved to Philadelphia and began Mr. Stewart's Cheshire Fox Hounds.

In 1902, Redmond Sr. married Katharine Latimer Small; 1,200 guests were invited to their wedding at old St. John's Episcopal Church in York, Pennsylvania. Four children came later: Latimer Small Stewart, Josephine Stewart Finney, Redmond Con-

Redmond Conyngham Stewart, 1931

Katharine Small Stewart, 1931

*Redmond Stewart Jr., on Vaudeville after the finish of the 1934 Maryland Grand
National. His brother, Latimer, is on the far right next to their uncle, Lurman Stewart*

yngham Stewart Jr., and Cassandra Steven Cassatt. The family
hunted – Katharine hunted side-saddle well into her 70s – and
shot and played tennis and golf together.

Redmond Sr.'s priorities are revealed by a letter he wrote to
Redmond Jr. before the latter began Harvard Law School. The first
part of the letter exhorts his son to study and pay attention to
his duty. The second part reads, "I went to luncheon with (name
removed) yesterday regarding your attending the Harvard Law
School. I told him you wanted one thing – to come down and ride
in the Maryland Hunt Race next spring. He said you would find
the professors in absolute sympathy with you and would tell you to
go ahead."

Redmond Jr. went on to win the Maryland Grand National in 1934 on his brother-in-law's horse and he rode in six Maryland Hunt Cups, finishing third three times. He married Ann Cochran, and they had four children: Redmond III, Kathy, Nina, and Ann. They grew up in an old stone house on the property where the Maryland Grand National is run every year and the family tradition of riding and hunting continued. There were always horses in the barn, and in 1968, one of those horses, Haffaday, won the Hunt Cup for Stewart with Louis "Paddy" Neilson riding.

Redmond Stewart Jr. after winning the 1934 Maryland Grand National. His sister, Sanna Cassatt, accepted the trophy for her husband, Alexander Cassatt.

Chapter Four

Like the Stewarts, the Fenwick family name has been associated with riding, training, and foxhunting in Maryland for more than 100 years. Charlie's grandfather, G. Bernard Fenwick, rode in the 1909 Hunt Cup and owned some horses that were contenders on the timber racing circuit. Charlie's father, Charles C. "Cuppy" Fenwick, also owned race horses and taught his five sons to ride and to foxhunt. Charlie got his first pony at seven years old and began to hunt soon after that.

As a teenager, Charlie and his brothers had the opportunity to absorb knowledge from their uncle, Bobby Fenwick. Among the many winning horses Bobby Fenwick trained was Jay Trump. Working around his uncle's stables while in high school, Charlie got to know Tommy Smith, who was not only Jay Trump's jockey for the Grand National, but also won the Maryland Hunt Cup five times.

Charlie worked galloping horses for various stables during holidays from school, notably at Belmont Park for Winkie Cocks. Charlie vividly remembers getting run off with at Belmont one day. Fortunately, he lost control on the far side of the track on a misty morning. By the time he came back around the turn and into sight, Charlie had the horse in hand and responded blandly to Winkie's questions that, yes, the horse seemed to go just fine.

Although Charlie was glad to have a chance to ride on the flat, he wanted to be a jockey over fences. In the U.S., there are two forms of steeplechase racing: timber and hurdle. A timber race is run over solid rail fences. These were originally used – and in many cases still are – to keep horses and cows in a field. Foxhunters would naturally come upon and jump them during a hunt. Built of solid wood, they are high and unyielding. In a hurdle race, the fences are built of brush, which is soft enough that a horse can sweep through the top without injury.

Charlie wanted to ride in timber races, not only because of family tradition and because it was a natural extension of his interest in hunting, but also because it is primarily an amateur sport in this country.

"It was the only thing I could do because I wasn't the caliber to be pro," he explains. "And I'd always have a weight problem." At five feet, 10 inches, he weighed around 155 pounds in high school.

Charlie began riding in races when he was 17. One of his early races was on a horse owned by Redmond Stewart Jr. "That was a wonderful thing, because everyone wants the best rider to get on his horse," Charlie once told an interviewer. "Instead, Mr. Stewart just said I should go out there and have a good time and learn all I could. That really meant a lot. The better horse you ride, the better your abilities get. If you get lucky enough to find a good horse, then your learning curve quickly develops with experience."

He rode in any race he could get a mount for, but didn't have much success until Hugh O'Donovan asked Charlie to ride his horse Café. O'Donovan was a former Master of Fox Hounds and had ridden in many races himself. He had Charlie start out hunting Café and O'Donovan remembered one of the first days vividly: "I had the field, and Charlie was on Café. We were in one of the fields right where Charlie lives now, and a deer suddenly came out. Charlie was jumping a line fence, and there was the deer right beside him jumping the same fence one panel down.

"The whole field saw it; it couldn't have been funnier. Café jumped like a stag with the deer, and that was really part of the beginning. We thought if he could stand training, we'd race him. He did pretty well, but I remember the first time out he had a horrible fall. It was the John Rush Streett Memorial race, and Charlie was riding him and they fell at the fourth fence. That was same race where Jay Griswold and two others were pretty close coming into the third fence, and all three of them flipped. Luckily, no one got hurt, and none of the horses were hurt, but it was pretty spectacular to see."

Charlie rode Café for three seasons, and they began to win some races. Around the same time Stuart S. Janney Jr. asked Charlie to ride his horse Arno, and it was on that horse that Charlie had his first sanctioned win at the Manor race in 1970. That year he also rode for the first time in the Hunt Cup on Arno, who ran well until the 16th fence; he fell there, but scrambled up with Charlie still aboard, and they finished the race.

In 1970, Charlie and Ann married and soon decided that they wanted to train horses as a business. Ann's mother stopped foxhunting at about that time, and Ann's father, Redmond Stewart Jr., was not riding as much. The Stewarts had barn space, and Josh Gill, their groom, had time on his hands. The young Fenwicks were able to work out an arrangement with Ann's parents to use the barn to begin, on a very small scale, training horses. Ann was a competent rider and had always liked watching races, but she didn't want to race herself, excepting the Old-Fashioned point-to-point hosted by the Green Spring Hounds. Training suited her better.

Charlie and Ann learned largely by trial and error, drawing from their accumulated knowledge and getting help from family and friends. The only formal training experience they acquired came from spending time with Jonathan Sheppard.

Sheppard, an Englishman, is a top trainer based in Pennsylvania. He is, in Charlie's words, a first-class horseman: "He is straightforward, well-educated, and you always know he is telling the truth."

In 1971, the Fenwicks were working with a horse named Happy Orphan that belonged to Charlie's father. They felt that he was better than his results were indicating, and so they sent him to Sheppard, going along to watch and learn themselves.

They learned a great deal from Sheppard, including what goals to set for a horse and how to achieve them, as well as how to work as a team themselves. Virtually all of the decisions with regard to their horses were mutually agreed upon; Charlie describes it as a partnership in the finest sense of the word.

They had their share of success and failure in the early days, exemplified in their results on the day of the 1973 Maryland Grand National. Charlie won the big race on Happy Orphan, but the horse cut his stifle on a fence and came back lame, thereby precluding competition in the Hunt Cup the following week. That disappointment was compounded in the next race when Charlie fell riding a horse named Devil's Lancer and broke his collarbone. However, that setback actually brought positive results, because, with Charlie out for a while, Ann was forced to learn to gallop race horses, and she has been galloping them ever since.

Charlie and Ann in the paddock before the Manor Race in 1973.

At that time the Fenwicks also were working with a Chilean mare named Minaccia, owned by Colonel Paul Wimert. They trained her with the understanding that they would not charge for board but would keep half of the money she made. Without an established record to attract owners, they often offered that sort of arrangement to prospective clients. As Ann recalls, "We were starting from nowhere and we were just desperately looking for action. Minaccia ran more than 30 times for us over hurdle fences and in timber races. She got us going and she was a marvelous mare."

"She was a lot of fun," Charlie agrees, "but I remember that she could sense when a race wasn't going to go her way. If she thought she could win, she would come in exhausted from the effort, but if she thought she was going to be beaten, she would make little or no effort. Fort Devon beat her a couple times, and I think after that when she even saw him in the paddock she would decide not to try in the race."

The year 1974 started off auspiciously. Charles C. Fenwick III was born in January, younger brother to Beth, who was two at the time, and Charlie had taken a job with the Baltimore-based stock brokerage Alex. Brown & Sons. The Fenwicks had Happy Orphan and Minaccia in training and decided to try to find one or two more horses to train.

Charlie's mother, Mrs. Donald Culver, was interested in buying a horse, so when the Fenwicks heard that Sheppard was going to Argentina that winter to buy horses, they asked him to look for one for her that would be a suitable timber prospect. Sheppard brought back two horses: Dosdi ($10,000) and Alvaro ($11,000). When offered a choice, the Fenwicks took Dosdi, liking his looks. Ben Nevis would complete their stable.

Chapter Five

When Ben Nevis came to the U.S. in 1974, he became known officially as Ben Nevis II, because the Jockey Club ruled that he was the second horse of that name to race in this country. He arrived in Maryland unheralded on a Saturday soon after Labor Day. The next morning there was a gathering at the barn to have a look at the new addition. Stewart came out of the house dressed in his pajamas and white terry-cloth bathrobe, his usual Sunday morning garb. His wife Ann, Charlie and Ann with the children, and the groom Josh Gill, were all there. Charlie and Gill went into the stall to tack up Ben Nevis. They immediately realized they had a challenge on their hands. The horse didn't want to be caught or held, or to stand quietly. It was a wrestling match, but at last they got the tack on and led him out of the barn. Charlie got a leg up and Ben Nevis began bucking. He kept it up and then reared and the surprised Charlie could not stay on.

Gill caught the horse, and Charlie picked himself up. Puzzled, they tried again. This time, before throwing Charlie, Ben Nevis hit him in the face as he reared, adding a bloody nose to Charlie's grievances. Fortunately, the terry-cloth bathrobe was on hand, and Charlie used a corner of it to mop up the blood.

Ann remembers the occasion well: "Oh, the color of it all that first day! It was really something. Charlie going out there, and we were all so excited – here was the new toy. And then Charlie getting thrown off, and my father saying, 'Charlie, I'd get on him but I'm too old!' And the flap – you can imagine! You get this new horse and you've told everyone about it, and Bobby Fenwick approved it and *nobody* can ride him. I don't know how they even got the bridle on that first day."

As far as they could see, there was nothing particularly wrong or, for that matter, particularly right, with the horse. He looked to them to be just another horse. His hind end was a little bigger than his front end, and he was not powerful looking or at all impressive. There was no way to guess that he would become a champion and no reason to think he would be such an intractable problem.

Certainly, there was little speculation about his potential that first day; at issue was how to stay on him. Charlie tried for a third time and was deposited on the ground once again. Disappointed and disgruntled, the whole group repaired to the house and sent the horse back to his stall. They immediately telephoned Michael Bannister to, as Charlie says, "Ask him what the hell is the matter with this horse, and what do we do now?"

Bannister wasn't home, and even when reached later, he did not have any answers for them. Being a gentleman, he did not point out that he had told Stewart in the first place that the horse was a problem.

It was not an encouraging start, and the situation became only marginally better in the following weeks. Charlie and Gill discovered that if they put Ben Nevis on a lunge line and worked him for about five minutes to warm him up and allow him to get used to the feel of the saddle, then Charlie could get on him. But once up, Charlie remembers, "He was always tense, always right on the muscle, never relaxed, like something was really bothering him." Charlie tried every trick he knew to get the horse to unwind, but nothing made a difference. The horse was like the Strawberry Roan in the old song that Charlie and his brothers used to listen to when they were kids.

Opinions were solicited from various family members. Bobby Fenwick looked at Ben Nevis but offered no ideas. He called in his daughter Carol, a trainer herself, and the Fenwick's longtime groom, Herb Madden, for their opinions. They had difficulty even catching Ben Nevis in the stall, much less working with him. Their reaction was the same as everyone else's. Carol says, "We didn't know what on earth was wrong with him except that he was a very difficult horse."

A veterinarian was consulted and he looked closely at the horse. Ben Nevis tensed and shied away when a person simply ran a hand down his back. The vet's best judgment was that the horse really had a back problem and might have to be put down.

But Charlie wasn't ready to give up. He turned to his brother Bruce for help. Bruce, also a trainer, had more time to work with Ben Nevis and more help in his stable to ascertain whether the horse really had a medical problem. Also, the Fenwicks did not know how much schooling the gelding had had, so it was a question of taking the time to experiment and learn about him. They tried schooling him over jumps on a lunge line and found that he jumped well. He could jump at speed and didn't make mistakes. However, he would not cooperate with a rider on his back. "I used to lunge him over jumps for Mr. Stewart to show him I was doing something with the horse, and he used to get all excited," Bruce Fenwick confesses. "I didn't dare tell him I couldn't get Ben to do that when I was riding him!"

The weeks went by with Ben Nevis continuing to buck and plunge, and with the mystery of his behavior still unsolved. However, the group working with him began to feel confident that he did not have any physical injury, and Ben Nevis seemed to be getting more used to being handled. Finally, they got fed up with doing nothing with him and decided to try him in the hunting field. The Children's Hunt after Thanksgiving, less challenging and less formal than other hunts, was chosen as the best place to begin. Bruce agreed, with some trepidation, to ride.

Jeep Cochran was Field Master and she remembers the day well: "I was trying to keep the field in some order. There were masses of children there, and then Bruce appeared from the woods and he did have his hands full. In fact, I'd have to say his horse was out of control. He was just going in circles and he sort of annihilated the back of the field – he didn't stay very long."

Bruce's memory of the day is also very clear: "It was like a rodeo; I attempted to get on Ben and stayed on for about 40 yards and then got bucked off. I got back on, and we battled for a while and finally got to the hunt. And it was a disaster – he lunged and bolted through the woods. We didn't get anywhere and we never tried it again. I think after that there was a lot of discussion about putting him down. The consensus was that he had some talent but was just unusable. He was no treat to ride – very dangerous, in fact."

Ben Nevis went back to Charlie, who continued to work with him. "He didn't jump well when I was riding him," Charlie remembers. "He always acted like something was bothering him. We were always trying to make him go slowly, but he wouldn't relax and he always pulled like hell. After 15 minutes on him, my arms would be screaming." Finally, Charlie told his father-in-law "that he ought to just cut his losses and give the horse away and write it off. And then the two of us had a real blowout."

If Charlie was stubborn, so was Stewart. Both men had definite opinions and they aired them. Strong words were exchanged. Redmond Stewart had determined that Ben Nevis was going to be trained and ridden, and he was not going to take anyone's advice to the contrary. On Charlie's side, he wouldn't allow the horse to be given to someone else to train, ultimately deciding that, "Either I'd break the horse or the horse would break me, and Mr. Stewart would like it either way."

Charlie and Ben Nevis struggled with each other all through the winter. Even leading him was difficult. Charlie says, "He'd pull on the shank so hard, it was almost as though he had claustrophobia." It was clear that hunting was not an option, so Charlie exercised him six days a week. Usually, Ben Nevis would jog a mile and gallop two miles, which meant nine times around the small straw track that the Fenwicks used when the ground was frozen. With the horse pulling the whole time, as he did for his entire career, it became a miserable routine.

As time passed, two things made a great difference in handling Ben Nevis. One was taking the time to lunge him before Charlie tried to get on. It seemed to calm the horse and get him used to the feel of the saddle. The other important factor in achieving progress was the influence of Josh Gill. He had worked with horses all his life, and by then he was getting on in years. As Ann notes, "He could do anything with Ben; he just about talked with him. He had a lovely attitude and he loved the horse. He loved all the horses, and with Ben, if we had had someone rough or slapping him around, it sure wouldn't have helped."

Charlie adds, "He was one of the nicest human beings who ever lived, just a genuinely nice man every day, and he did have a way with that horse."

It was Gill who discovered a foolproof way to catch Ben Nevis. The groom chewed Red Man tobacco, and one day he took a package of it out while working around Ben Nevis. The horse began nosing into his hands, and Gill offered him the tobacco. Ben Nevis promptly took some and from that time on became his chewing companion. But Ben Nevis liked only Red Man; other brands didn't have the same appeal.

Rita Goolsby, who has worked for the Fenwicks for many years, remembers that when she needed to bring Ben Nevis in from a field, she didn't bother to try to entice him with oats – she would go straight to the supply of Red Man to be sure she could catch the horse.

Chapter Six

That first winter of 1974-1975 seemed long for Charlie and Ann. Not only was riding Ben Nevis a daily unpleasant chore, but also having to listen to Redmond Stewart's comments about the situation didn't help matters. He loved to say things like, "Yes, I gave Charlie a toy a child couldn't break, idiot-proof!"

Finally, spring came and with it time to make a decision. The horse was fit and there was no point in training him if he never raced. With much forethought and a great deal of apprehension, Charlie and Ann decided to enter Ben Nevis in a flat race, choosing the Goshen Hunt, a small Maryland point-to-point, held in early March.

Charlie recalls, "Frankly, we expected the worst, but we had to run him – that was what he was there for, so we chose that race just for the education, to learn something about him. Also, it wasn't a very formal meet, and you could get away with murder. We were able to get permission to skip the paddock altogether, which was necessary because we thought Ben just might go berserk from all the excitement. We saddled him up in the van, and when they said 'Riders up!' we were off in the middle of the field somewhere. Ann gave me a leg up, and Josh was holding him and he did go crazy, but we managed to get him to the start. The race went off, and I think it was the roughest race I ever rode in. There were eight in the field, and it just seemed like horses were careening off of each other. We bumped some horses and it was chaotic, but the race was only about a mile and a quarter. With maybe a half a mile to go, Ben went to the front. He won it pretty easily, but I tell you it was a nerve-racking experience."

"It was also pretty damn exciting," Ann adds. "We were all expecting the worst, and here was this horse that we thought was a crazy maniac winning the race!"

The Fenwicks were thrilled with the day's results. Not only had they not expected Ben Nevis to win, but also they genuinely had feared that he might take off and run through the crowd. They were very relieved that Charlie had been able to control him in a race, and they were pleased by his speed.

Because of their trepidation about the outcome of the race, they had advised Redmond Stewart not to attend. When Charlie and Ann telephoned him later to give him the news, he was predictably excited, but with some smugness mixed in. That night he went to a party and, in his usual fashion, proceeded to tell all of the other guests about the race and to take credit for the result.

At this point in Ben Nevis's training, it wasn't clear that he could jump in a race. He would go along when he was schooling on a lunge line, but with a rider he seemed to go too fast and was almost unmanageable. Nonetheless, the Fenwicks decided to see what he could do over hurdles. They picked out a race at Middleburg two weeks after his surprising victory at Goshen. In preparation, Charlie schooled Ben Nevis at Bruce's farm, where they discovered to their surprise that he didn't brush through the hurdles, he jumped right over them.

"We found out, 'Hey, he's jumping way over top of them,' and we were going pretty fast and he was doing really well. In fact, the faster we were going, the better he was jumping!'" Charlie explains. "So Ann and I talked it over and thought, 'Well, we're in the timber business, not in the hurdle business, and we've got to do something with him, so let's run him in a timber race and see what happens.'"

It was a risk. They knew he had some speed, but the two big uncertainties were whether he had jumping ability in a race and whether he could be controlled.

They decided to enter him in the Louis Leith Cup in Middleburg. This was a very different meeting from the small country races at Goshen. There were some good horses competing and a sizeable audience. Getting Ben Nevis ready for the race was a task that required careful planning and close attention. The routine for preparing him varied little throughout most of his career. He was always strung up, very much on his toes, so the Fenwicks virtually always tacked him up in the barn or in the van to avoid a battle in the paddock. Additionally, they tried to arrange things so that Charlie spent very little time on the horse's back; they always tried to avoid making two circuits of the paddock. They would ask permission for Charlie to go around only once, but if it was not granted, they omitted one circle anyway; getting reprimanded by the officials was a lot less of a problem than handling Ben Nevis for any length of time.

Josh Gill always went to Ben Nevis's races, accompanied by another groom, Donald Howard. They would prepare the horse together, and then Gill or Howard would take him to the paddock.

Ann says, "For the first few races, I remember watching Ben and thinking, 'My God, he's going to jump over the snow fence!' Everyone would say how washy he was and all that stuff, but he was just getting himself ready. After a while we figured if we put Nipper, my hunter, in front of him, he wouldn't go all over the place because, you see, he wasn't really crazy – he just was nervous and on his toes and ready to get on with it. So I'd ride Nipper, and he would settle him some, but boy, Ben was a live wire in the paddock, especially at first. Josh was old by then and not too steady, and yet somehow he'd always get that horse around. And I tell you it would just take your breath away to watch."

The Middleburg meet was held March 23, 1975. Peter Winants, writing for *The Chronicle of the Horse*, was there and gave this account of the race:

> "This was an excellent 3-mile timber race, and most thought that David Robinson's Lost Lamb, Skip Brittle up, would prevail. The confident pair sailed along in front, jumping well, and gaily turned back challenges by Portobelo III (Paddy Neilson) and Gun Mount (Turney McKnight), while Believe the Price (Jon Ruhsam) fell at the fence in front of the stands. Suddenly, a surprising newcomer, Redmond C. Stewart's Ben Nevis, friend Fenwick up, moved to the frontrunner approaching the last, and landed in front over that fence. The Marylanders increased their margin through the stretch to win by two or three lengths. Ben Page, owned by Hunter Lott and a first-time starter over timber, was an impressive third under Duncan Patterson. . . At Middleburg, Ben Nevis added jumping ability to his repertoire, and he's unquestionably a 'comer.'"

As Charlie remembers, it was a pretty good race and they won it easily, despite a messy point early on. Someone up front made a mistake at the second fence, and when Ben Nevis and Charlie arrived there, they were confronted with a pileup. Ben Nevis had to crawl over another horse to get out of the jam, and apparently he struck himself in the process. He pulled himself together to win, but after the race he had some swelling in a leg. Not wanting to aggravate the injury further, and also reasoning that it was not wise to push him too much too soon, the Fenwicks gave Ben the rest of the season off.

Making plans for the spring of 1976, Charlie and Ann decided to aim for one big race with Ben Nevis. They had the impression that he might not be very sound because of the tendon strain he had sustained at Middleburg, and they still didn't know if he could jump big fences. Accordingly, they chose a conservative path, planning to race him once in late May at Fair Hill. Not only were the fences smaller there than on some other courses they considered, but also no one would know him. That meant that they could place a substantial bet, which might provide a nice bonus.

That was a good idea in theory, but Ben Nevis wasn't like other horses. He lived on his nerves, so he became fitter much faster than an average horse. By the end of March he was so fit that the Fenwicks realized they couldn't wait for two months to race him; therefore, they entered him in Mr. Stewart's Cheshire Bowl in Unionville, Pennsylvania. (The race was named for Plunkett Stewart, Ann's great uncle.)

Five horses started the race, which was run over three miles and included 19 fences. A mare named Mid Clare had been getting a lot of attention and was considered the horse to beat with Bruce Davidson, an Olympic rider, up.

Oliphant, ridden by Michael Plumb, also an Olympian, took the lead early, and the rest were packed together close behind. He fell behind Ben Nevis and Mid Clare approaching the "in and out." At the fourth from last fence, Curt Crossman on Danny's Brother closed in, and the three horses jumped head to head with two more fences to go. Ben Nevis took out some rails at the next, and there was an even sprint to the last fence. He gained in the air and crossed the line a length in front, giving the crowd an exciting finish. Mid Clare was a close third to Danny's Brother. While the quality of the horses was not outstanding, it was a competitive race and Ben Nevis won it easily without being fully extended.

Dosdi finished second in the following race, so it was a good day all around for the Fenwicks. Their initial fear that Ben Nevis would prove to be unsound was unfounded, so they entered him in the John Rush Streett Memorial at the Manor races two weeks later, his first sanctioned race.

The Streett Memorial is a race for horses that have not won two sanctioned races, and that year none of the other entrants had ever won a timber race. At the second fence, Crazy Stripes parted ways with his rider, Bruce Fenwick. The rest of the pack stayed pretty tight until the ninth. There, Pat's Gamble fell hard, sending rider Warrington "Warry" Gillet to the hospital, and interfering with Thomas Voss on Super Buper, who fell also. It was left to J.B. Secor on Green Rd., owned by J. Fife Symington, to challenge Ben Nevis. Secor gave Charlie a run for his money coming into the last fence, which the two horses jumped together, but in the stretch Ben Nevis moved ahead three lengths and won easily. The Fenwicks were further pleased that day by Charlie's second-place finish in the next race on Semington, Wallace Lanahan Jr.'s horse.

One week later was the Maryland Grand National, and Ben Nevis was entered in the Benjamin H. Murray Memorial, the second race on the day's card. The race did not get off to a good start. In the paddock, Moe Green went over backward, throwing his head back violently and cutting rider Buzzy Hannum's face so badly that he had to be taken off and sewed up. The crowd's sentiments lay with 62-year-old Stitler Vipond, who had resumed racing that season after a sabbatical of many years. He had won several point-to-points on the Delaware Valley circuit earlier that spring, and in the Murray Memorial he was aboard his own horse, Durock.

There were not great expectations for Ben Nevis, largely due to a rumor that he had gone lame after his race the previous week. However, as soon as the flag dropped, he proved how fit he was by going off to a commanding lead which was never contested. An unfortunate accident brought Durock down at the ninth fence, sending Vipond briefly to the hospital. Louis "Paddy" Neilson on Semington attempted to challenge Ben Nevis in the final mile and would have been second, but they fell at the next-to-last fence.

The Chronicle of the Horse reported, "Though Ben Nevis was never pressed, and was, indeed, under severe restraint for the entire race, he showed considerable class in his jumping and galloping. He obviously could have covered the course in faster time than the 6:06 which he recorded, but just how much faster is the question. Ben Nevis is obviously not an easy horse to ride, and Charlie Fenwick deserves great praise for bringing him home a winner two weeks in a row."

Charlie and Ben Nevis before the Benjamin H. Murray Memorial Race in 1976.

Charlie remembers that the race went wire-to-wire, that the ground was rock-hard, and that his horse was head and shoulders better than everyone else's that day. "Here we had a horse which had run in four timber races and was yet to be defeated," he recalls. "It was getting pretty heady." Excitement and expectations were growing.

45

Finally, the Fair Hill race came around. By then everyone knew Ben Nevis's record, so there wasn't any money to be made betting that day. He would be racing against Jacko, by far the best horse against which he had been pitted. An early lead was taken by Gabby S., ridden by Duncan Patterson. Charlie kept Ben Nevis off the pace until there was about a mile to go, and then he moved to the front. Jacko fought to keep up, with Wendy Jones driving him on, but Ben Nevis surged ahead and won by an easy four lengths.

Although Jacko may have been a little past his prime, he was still competitive. Therefore, at that point the Fenwicks began to have some confidence that Ben Nevis was actually a good horse. The racing fraternity also began to recognize him as a contender, and he started to receive attention. In addition, Charlie and Ann were learning an enormous amount during this period, gradually gaining confidence in their own abilities. Their readiness to learn, their patience, and their tenacity made up in large measure for their inexperience.

In a way, that inexperience may have been a positive thing with regard to Ben Nevis's training. Charlie said years later that he believed, "At that stage I had just enough ability to control Ben, but not enough to mess him up. I think if he came along today, I would be much more adamant about forcing him to do things our way, and that would have ruined him. He just had a tremendous amount of raw talent that we developed. But we didn't teach him much. The challenge was controlling that talent."

Ben Nevis approached fences well, as though he knew exactly what he was doing. "Ben just didn't meet fences wrong," Charlie asserts. "He jumped them with a lot of power and speed, but he wasn't rash. He would get back on his hocks, fold his front legs tightly, use his back, and tuck up behind. You felt like you were on a launching pad sometimes. He was courageous, and I think he loved it. He relished the running, the racing. I always thought he was running on his nerves, which isn't a good thing generally, but he liked to be in front when he was running over here."

It was lucky timing for the Fenwicks that they had Dosdi and Ben Nevis in their stable at the same time. With two good horses to work with, they did not push either one too hard, and the couple eventually developed a schedule of running Ben Nevis in the spring and Dosdi in the fall.

That spring Charlie won the Virginia Gold Cup, for the first time, on Semington. Although the race was not a particularly competitive one, the Gold Cup is a prestigious meet and therefore it was a thrill for Charlie and Ann to have their first victory there. In the fall Dosdi won four races, which brought to eight the number of sanctioned timber races that the Fenwicks won in 1976. They had a strong stable and were beginning to establish themselves in the racing community.

Chapter Seven

In December 1976, Charlie slipped when getting onto a tractor and sliced open his leg. He received more than 50 stitches, which kept him from riding for weeks. Ben Nevis therefore had to be worked on a lunge line, and the Fenwicks feared that might set him back. However, they discovered that he was the type of horse that became fit practically on his own. By April 1977, Charlie was telling reporters that Ben Nevis was "the fastest horse I've ever ridden, definitely the best we've got and the best we've ever had, and he's our big Hunt Cup hope."

There was great excitement about the upcoming season. The idea that they had a good shot at winning the Maryland Hunt Cup was heady for the Fenwicks and the Stewarts. That goal sustained Charlie through a rigorous late winter and early spring. Ann, pregnant with their youngest daughter Emily, wasn't riding at all. Therefore, Charlie was up with the sun to ride four horses every morning before work. He says, "I kept telling myself, 'Maybe it will be that morning when I got up and it was 10-below and I didn't thaw out until after lunch – that morning that I went out and the other guy didn't – that will help me win the race.'"

Ben Nevis's first race of the season was the Howard County Cup, held on a cold damp day in early April. The ground was wet, the competition uninspired. Ben Nevis went to the front at the start and won easily in a three-horse field. Jay Griswold, riding his own horse Coney Island, was second, and Roman Blaze, ridden by his owner, Art Williams, was pulled up.

Three weeks later was the Grand National point-to-point. The conditions were ideal, with firm, dry ground on a beautiful, sunny day. Although Ben Nevis was favored to win, he would have to earn the victory: Paddy Neilson was riding Kinloch for George T. Weymouth; J.B. Secor was on Pat's Gamble, owned by Harry L. Burkheimer Jr.; Perfect Cast, Audrey Riker's mare, was ridden by Turney McKnight; and Buzzy Hannum was on Burnmac, winner of the Maryland Grand National and the 1974 Hunt Cup.

The account of the race in *The Maryland Horse* began by noting that, "Redmond C. Stewart Jr.'s Ben Nevis II isn't impressive in the paddock before a race. Hot and difficult, it takes a strong man to walk him. He is small, too, next to the other jumpers and his dark chestnut coat drips water. There is no indication of the athletic ability which is locked in his compact body. However, over the 18 fences of the Grand National point-to-point. . . the 8-year-old gelding was a giant killer, a David among Goliaths."

The going was very fast due to dry weather. Ben Nevis took the lead at the start, with Burnmac and Pat's Gamble close behind, followed by Kinloch and Perfect Cast. The horses held these positions and were evenly spaced with about three lengths between them until they turned to head for Gill Fenwick's barns. At that point Pat's Gamble closed in and Perfect Cast moved up. Crossing the driveway about a third of a mile from the finish, Ben Nevis still led, but Secor urged Pat's Gamble to Charlie's side. In Secor's words, "At the last fence we were going so fast that if we hadn't met that fence just right, it would have been all over," Secor says. "But

*Ben Nevis jumping second to last fence in the 1973 Grand
National. Pat's Gamble with J.B. Secor follows.*

we did. My horse came back to me and jumped it just right. It was
fun, I tell you."

Despite Pat's Gamble's terrific jump, Ben Nevis pulled away
in the stretch to win by a length and a half, setting a new course
record.

"He was pushed at the end," Charlie remembers, "which got
him to set a record that day and he still was not fully extended.
That was a surprise. . . although the ground was very hard and that
made the speed much faster. After the last fence I realized Pat's
Gamble wasn't going to pass him, so I wasn't riding him out as
hard as I could've been. I think maybe the others weren't trying,
probably using the race as prep for the Hunt Cup. One of the reasons I think I've won so many Grand Nationals is that often horses
are given a schooling over the big fences if it looks like they don't

DOUGLAS LEES

Redmond Stewart Jr. after the Grand National win, 1977.

have a good chance of winning. But you were never going to do that with Ben Nevis. You couldn't 'give' him a race; he was always going to try."

One week later was the Maryland Hunt Cup, always held on the last Saturday in April. It was a gorgeous spring day, but the Fenwicks weren't thinking about sunny skies. The course inspires a healthy respect, if not plain fear, in all who contemplate riding over it. And those who watch someone they love try to conquer the four-mile, 22-fence course often suffer terrible anxiety.

"It gives me nightmares," Ann says. "It is unbelievably difficult. You just don't know what is going to happen on a given day."

The Hunt Cup fences are notorious for their height and solidity. They are made from rounded chestnut rails, up to 18 inches in circumference, driven into locust posts buried four feet into the ground, and virtually unbreakable. The third fence is formidable: five rails with the top logs weighing close to 85 pounds and measuring four feet, nine inches straight up and down. It is often the highest fence a jockey and his horse have ever jumped up to that time, and it can come as a shock to both. Also, crowds always gather at that fence, and the competitors can feel as if they're jumping into people, an unsettling sensation. Many hopes have been dashed at this fence. The 13th is like the third and both have been called "Union Memorial" fences, referring to the local hospital where injured riders are taken. At four feet, 10 inches, the 16th is the tallest; approached on the uphill, it jumps even higher. By the time horses reach it, they already have run three miles, and the pace usually picks up by then.

The dreaded third fence of the Maryland Hunt Cup. Charlie coming off Happy Orphan in 1974 – neither horse nor rider was hurt.

"At that point in the race," Charlie says, "it becomes a question of survival."

Each fence has its stories. In 1935, Mrs. Marion DuPont Scott's Trouble Maker over-jumped the 17th fence and somersaulted, breaking his neck. His rider, unhurt, wept over the fallen horse's body. Mrs. Scott went home and tore down all of her timber fences and swore she would never run a horse over timber again. Trouble Maker was buried where he fell.

Charlie and Ann had a great deal of confidence in Ben Nevis by this time, but they were conscious of his lack of experience, and, too, they still didn't know him well enough to predict how he would react to the course. "You say a horse can do it and you believe it, but you never know," Charlie says. "Even if some horses can do it physically, some can't mentally. I remember riding Minac- cia in 1976, and I know she began to realize halfway through the race, 'Hell, these fences could really kill you!' She just lost heart, and I had to drag her around the last half of the course."

Ann adds, "I think it takes a lot of courage to go around in front; you almost want an older horse to give you a lead."

Ben Nevis was expected to win, but some thought that his speed might prove to be his undoing, reasoning that if he hit one of the unyielding fences going that fast, he would be brought down. In the nine-horse field, Kinloch, Neilson riding again, seemed to be the horse to beat, while the mare Perfect Cast, with McKnight up, also figured to give Ben Nevis a tough race.

Spectators and journalists covering the race were, as usual, struck by Ben Nevis's appearance before the start. Peter Winants wrote, "Ben Nevis hardly looked the part of a Hunt Cup winner. He was saddled in solitary splendor at a nearby barn, and when brought to the paddock, the liver-colored chestnut was washy and high-headed, prancing like a steel spring, on the verge of erupt- ing."

While the crowd watched tensely, Charlie got Ben to the start without mishap. The start was clear, but the course began to take its toll at the third fence when Foxbrook Farm's Raford Boy hooked a rail and fell, bringing rider R.P.S. "Buzzy" Hannum down with him. Count Turk, owned by Melinda Rogers, was ahead briefly coming into the fourth fence, but he hit it and tossed rider Don Yovonovich onto his ears before the pair went down. Ben Nevis set the pace, with Kinloch in second and Perfect Cast jumping easily in third. Michael Plumb, riding Koolabah for Samuel Wilcox III, fell at the ninth fence, and the first three horses increased their lead. Essex II, owned and ridden by Benjamin H. Griswold IV, was behind.

At the formidable 16th, Ben Nevis came close to disaster. He jumped badly and smashed the top rail. However, between his remarkable agility and Charlie's poised horsemanship, the pair regained their balance and raced on. Behind them, Kinloch also hit the 16th and wavered a bit, but Neilson was able to steady him and urge him up to Ben Nevis's quarters by the 18th fence.

Charlie told reporter Nancy Boyce, "The 18th is troublesome because horses are getting tired and it's not all that small. Kinloch was lapped on my quarters, and I wondered what would happen. We cleared it. Then I looked back and was surprised to see Kinloch, Perfect Cast, and Moon Meeting closer than I hoped they would be. I felt relieved when Kinloch went down at the 19th, but then Perfect Cast was coming to me over the 20th and 21st, which are board fences and smaller than the others."

The mare faltered at the last fence, but McKnight gathered her at the top of the stretch and drove to the finish. She was game and cut into Ben Nevis's lead, much to the crowd's excitement, but she couldn't get to him in time. Redmond Stewart's gelding won by a length, his time six seconds faster than Fort Devon's from the previous year.

"I've ridden this course five times, and it is always scary," Charlie said after the race. "However, Ben Nevis is the best horse I've been on. He became cautious when he found out how big the fences were. The drop on the other side surprised him, I think. Even though we led the whole way, it was exciting, because every time I tried to relax, someone would challenge us. And at the end

Turney made a terrific run at us and was closing a lot of ground, but we held on by a length."

Years later Charlie expressed his feelings about the race by saying, "Finally winning the bloody thing after dreaming about it for so long and trying several times was such a thrill. Accomplishing something you've aimed for is tremendously satisfying. . . it is exhilarating and at the same time sort of a blur; it all sort of happens despite you. For us, for most people in this sport, it is an accomplishment of a lifetime; it's an incredible feeling."

The Stewart and Fenwick clans were delighted and later met at the Hunt Ball to celebrate. "That is always fun," notes Charlie, "especially the chance to make a toast. Of course, for quite a while I always suffered from too much champagne before I got around to that, but it is then that you have a chance to say what the race meant to you and what happened, and I always enjoyed that. It is a great opportunity to thank all the people involved and reflect a little bit."

Naturally, after the race there was talk about the future for Ben Nevis, and in Charlie's mind the idea of trying for the big prize at Aintree began to take shape. However, it seemed premature to make such plans.

Ben Nevis had his usual summer of leisure before going back to work in the fall of 1977. He was now a considerably more quiet horse than the one who had arrived three years earlier. Constant handling by people with a real love and understanding of horses had made enormous changes in his demeanor.

Ann remembers with affection, "He trusted you in his stall. You could fool with his legs, and he would stand perfectly quietly. I really felt like you could put a child in there. He got to be a member of the family and seemed practically housebroken by the end."

However, his behavior with a rider up never really changed. The routine of lunging him before he was ridden was necessary throughout his career. In the fall, after months off, he was particularly fractious. There would be several mornings of rearing and plunging before he calmed down and grew used to Charlie on his back again. The winter was cold and snowy, and Charlie had to plow a track in the snow in order to exercise Ben Nevis. It was miserable keeping him fit.

The 1978 spring season began with Ben Nevis's entry in the S. Lurman Stewart Memorial Challenge Trophy (named for another of Ann's great uncles) at the Elkridge-Harford meet in Maryland. Three days before the race, the Fenwicks had a big scare. On that Thursday, Ben Nevis was lame in his hind leg. The couple's concern and disappointment were extreme. Charlie left work early in the afternoon to meet a veterinarian at the stables. The horse was obviously hurting, but the vet couldn't find a reason for it. They could do nothing but wait. By Saturday it appeared that time was all that was needed. To everyone's surprise and relief, the bizarre injury apparently had healed. Ben Nevis seemed as fit as ever and was taken to the races.

That scare was very unusual for Ben Nevis. He virtually never got sick and recovered from his rare injuries quickly. His blood count was always high, and vets used to say when they drew blood that it seemed to come out faster and was a richer color than that of other horses. After having worked with many horses after Ben Nevis, Ann still claims that she has never come across a healthier one.

Ben Nevis over the 12th fence of the Grand National in 1978.

There were only two other entries in the Stewart Memorial, Still in All, ridden by owner Turney McKnight, and Green Rd., ridden by Bruce Fenwick. McKnight took the lead early, and Ben Nevis jumped comfortably with him or just off his quarters until the 17th fence. There, Ben Nevis forged ahead to lead by two-plus lengths. Still in All tired coming into the finish, while Ben Nevis breezed up the hill to finish strongly, 10 lengths in front. Green Rd. was pulled up. It was a particularly satisfying result for Charlie, who had ridden his first winner at Elkridge-Harford in 1966. Although he had ridden there every year since, this was only his second victory at the meeting. "I'm pleased with the way he went,"

DOUGLAS LEES

*After the Grand National trophy presentation; Charlie
with his son, Charles C. Fenwick III.*

Charlie said after the race. "I wouldn't want to see him jump any better."

The Grand National followed in two weeks, and with Ben Nevis's record now 10-for-10, few questioned the outcome of the race. And, indeed, there were no surprises. On a bright spring day with the ground softened by midweek rain, the favorite led all the way. He was challenged only moderately by the rest of the field of five. Still in All stalked the leader by about two lengths throughout the race. Green Rd., ridden this time by Steve Secor, put in a bad jump at the fourth fence, and although he was able to move up to Ben Nevis briefly at the seventh, he was not jumping well and finally fell at the 17th. Moon Meeting, with Ross Pearce up, finished third, and Buzzy Hannum on Hammurabi III came in fourth, 10 lengths behind. It was an easy Grand National for Ben Nevis, but by this time everything seemed to be easy for him. He was up to any task Charlie asked of him.

However, at least one person there that day imagined another outcome. "Whenever I raced against Ben Nevis, I thought I might win because he was such an orangutan in the paddock," Turney McKnight admits. "He was covered with lather – his neck was a sight! And I was on Still in All in that race, who was the best horse I ever owned. He was 100 percent fit and sound and ran as well as he ever did. He jumped every fence perfectly, and he was a beaten animal by the second-to-last fence, when he did make a mistake."

McKnight had another chance the following week in the Hunt Cup. He was on Perfect Cast again, riding for Audrey Riker. Hunt Cup day, April 29, was clear and warm. Blossoms were out under blue skies, and a crowd of about 9,000 was there to see the action. As always, there was plenty of it both on and off the course. Ann's

DOUGLAS LEES

*Ann leading Nipper to the paddock before the Hunt Cup
with Donald Howard and Ben Nevis behind.*

hunter, Nipper, quieted Ben Nevis effectively in the paddock, re-
lieving some and disappointing others, all of whom expected his
usual antics. There was a strong sense of anticipation because the
idea had taken root that England might be the next step for the
Fenwick entry if he ran well that day. Also, a victory would mean
that Redmond Stewart could retire the Hunt Cup trophy, having
won the race twice before.

The ground was firm and fast. Ben Nevis took the lead at the
first fence, followed closely by Moon Meeting and Perfect Cast.
Handsome Daddy, ridden by Bruce Fenwick, was just behind. Navy
Davy, in the rear, blundered at the third fence, and Don Yovonovich
came off. By the fourth fence, Ben Nevis was four lengths ahead of
Perfect Cast. Behind them was Moon Meeting, followed by Handsome Daddy. After the fifth fence, the mare, urged by McKnight,
began her bid. She caught Ben Nevis and stayed with him, jump-

Ben Nevis with a tremendous leap over the 16th fence; Hunt Cup 1978.

DOUGLAS LEES

Charlie and Ben Nevis, on the left, outfinish Turney McKnight on Perfect Cast.

ing side by side until after the ninth, when he pulled ahead going downhill into the 10th. At the 11th fence, Perfect Cast trailed by two lengths, with Moon Meeting four lengths behind her. Handsome Daddy raced gamely but 10 lengths off the pace.

The crowd around the 13th quieted when the field approached, and then applauded in relief as all the horses negotiated the big fence. Charlie gave his horse a breather after the 14th, and Perfect Cast, taking advantage, reached Ben Nevis's quarters by the 17th fence. She pushed Ben Nevis hard, and he fumbled a little under the pressure, making his worst jumps over the 18th, 19th, and 20th fences. However, at the last fence he was two lengths ahead and quickened in the stretch to finish six lengths in front. The official time was 8:33³/₅, breaking the record set by Landing Party in 1971 by almost nine seconds.

"Turney had mapped out the best possible strategy," Charlie told *The Maryland Horse* after the race, "and he executed it the best way possible. His plan was to keep the pressure on me and see if Ben would make a mistake. The courage and resolution required to do something like that are enormous. I give Turney and the mare great credit. Who can say if Ben would have gone so fast if he hadn't had that pressure? She pushed him, and, in return, Ben carried her to a terrific performance."

It was a gallant race by a beautiful mare that had returned to competition after two bowed tendons and having taken time off to produce a foal. For her owner, Audrey Riker, the defeat was crushing. "Well," she said ruefully, "some people have been trying to win this race for 50 years. I have only been trying for 20."

There was another ingredient that factored prominently in Ben Nevis's record-breaking performance. Bruce Fenwick, as acting superintendent of the course, recently had bought a new roller and used it for the first time just before the race. "He didn't realize it," Charlie says, "but it packed down the sod so much that it was like Tufton Avenue out there. He wouldn't use that roller again because it is too dangerous to have that fast a course."

Despite his defeat, McKnight speaks of the race with great fondness: "It is a day I will never forget. The two of us raced (together) virtually the entire way. It was an incredible thing. My feeling was that these walls of fences were coming at me so fast. I remember I got a headache – the only time I remember that happening – from concentrating so hard. It was such an extreme experience. But something I remember so well was right after the finish when Charlie and I were alone for a minute heading back to the crowd. Charlie turned to me and said, 'Turney, nobody will ever know

Redmond Stewart, Jr. on right retiring the Hunt Cup trophy in 1978 with his wife, Ann beside him. Charlie is standing in front of his daughter, Beth.

what it was like out there.' And I think that is so revealing – Charlie is able to savor every moment of a race. He loves every moment; it is not just the winning. There are riders, you know, who only start savoring the experience in the winner's circle, but not Charlie. He has an awareness and an appreciation that is really rare. I'll never forget the way he said that then and the look on his face."

Ben Nevis had jumped boldly and brilliantly, with complete confidence. The tentative approach of the year before had been replaced by a verve and enthusiasm that were exhilarating to watch. He had done everything that had been asked of him; in 12 races he had won 12 times. He held the Grand National and the Hunt Cup records. He had retired the Maryland Hunt Cup trophy for his owner. There were no further goals to reach for in America.

65

Chapter Eight

When it was determined that Ben Nevis was completely sound after his Hunt Cup victory, the enthusiasm for a try at the English Grand National began to mount. There were three factors that weighed heavily in favor of an attempt at Aintree. First, Ben Nevis was a consistently superb jumper. Second, he was sound. Third, and most important, he was always going to give everything he had. Paddy Neilson recalls, "There was no surprise that they were talking about going to England. Ben was that outstanding and he definitely deserved to go. Maybe we didn't exactly expect them to win, but we certainly didn't regard it as a long shot. We all had a lot of confidence in the size of Ben's heart and in the size of Charlie's heart, and that is most of it right there."

The timing was propitious in the Fenwicks' personal lives. As a stockbroker, Charlie could not leave his clients for nine months. However, he had been thinking about changing his line of work, and this was a logical time to make a break. Charlie and his father discussed the possibility of going into business together. During the summer they decided that Charlie would leave Alex. Brown & Sons and join his father in the automobile business. That made the possibility of taking several months off to go to England far more realistic. Charlie could leave his current job in the fall and begin work for his father in the spring. Other important considerations included what to do with their house, their other horses in training, the children's schooling, living arrangements, and finding a trainer in England.

Outweighing all practical difficulties was the knowledge that this was an opportunity of a lifetime. Having one's horse win at Aintree has been a dream that has eluded men and women who seem to have everything else. John Hay "Jock" Whitney, with a fortune of reportedly a half-billion dollars at his command, tried for most of his life to win the English race. When he was 25 in 1929, he commissioned a top British trainer to develop a stable of steeplechasers for him. Although he entered horses in the Grand National year after year, the grand prize always escaped him. Once, asked about it on his return from yet another fruitless trip to Aintree, this man, heir to one of the largest private fortunes in the United States, shook his head sadly and replied, "Just can't seem to break my luck."

The Fenwicks and the Stewarts knew the odds were against them and that many significant obstacles lay ahead, but they couldn't turn down the chance to compete in the Grand National, no matter what they had to do to get there.

Once the decision to take Ben Nevis to England was made, the first step was to find a trainer. Charlie made a list of all those he knew by reputation, and he also called Jonathan Sheppard for advice and ideas. Sheppard suggested Captain Tim Forster, pointing out that Forster had won the Grand National in 1972, that he was always in the top 10 trainers, and that he might be willing to take on an amateur.

Charlie sent letters introducing himself to all of the trainers on his list. One, Fred Winter, had won the race twice as a jockey and had subsequently trained Jay Trump and 1966 winner Anglo. Winter's reply said in essence that he questioned whether an 11-year-old horse, as Ben Nevis would be by April 1979, could learn something new. Clearly, he was not eager, and Charlie was a little put off by his tone. Then Tim Forster called to say that he would be interested in talking to Charlie. Although the English trainer had never heard of Ben Nevis prior to receiving Charlie's letter, he thought that the idea of Ben Nevis coming to England was a fair one, reasoning that, "If a horse can win the Maryland Hunt Cup, he can obviously jump."

Months later, after Charlie and Ann were established in Forster's yard, the trainer recounted that when he had received Charlie's letter, he had taken it with him to a dinner party one night, showing it to his friends both to entertain them and to get their reaction because he had not made up his mind whether to answer. One of his friends put him up to calling Charlie, saying, "Go ahead and do it! See what this guy is about." That tipped the balance, and Forster made the call.

In June, Charlie flew to England, accompanied by his friend Jay Griswold. In many cases he simply telephoned the trainers to whom he had written and explained that he was in England and asked if he could drop by.

Fred Winter was the first with whom he spoke, and the trainer agreed to meet with him. Winter, however, made it clear from the outset that he was not enthusiastic about working together. "He was not rolling out the red carpet at all," Charlie recalls.

While Winter did show Charlie and Griswold around his yard, he punctuated the tour with pointed comments about Americans, claiming that they had a strange way of doing things and were difficult to get along with. He informed them that Tommy Smith's win on Jay Trump was "the most amazing performance. I told him exactly what to do the whole way round, and he did exactly what I had told him. . . and he won." Winter's implication was that the surprising thing was that Smith had followed his directions, not that he had won.

When Charlie contacted him, Fred Winter was at the top of his profession. He had little to gain by taking on Charlie and Ben Nevis. For him, the unlikely outcome of the horse succeeding was not worth the certain difficulties of dealing with amateurs, and American amateurs, at that. Therefore, Charlie's proposal received a cool reception and it was mutually agreed that Winter's was not the place for Ben Nevis.

Jay Griswold and Charlie visited Tim Forster's place next. His was a classic English racing yard, with the stables attached to the manor house, which is actually a comfortable cottage with a thatched roof. It looked nearly idyllic to the Americans' eyes. Forster had about 60 horses, and the place was clearly well run, exuding charm.

"We talked and he showed us around and then the three of us sat down to lunch," Charlie remembers. "Well, there was this girl there fixing lunch, and she put the food out and took it back and brought some more food out, and I realized Jay was looking at this girl in what I considered a most peculiar fashion. Finally, Jay says in his own classic way, 'Don't I know you?' And the girl says, 'Yes, you know me,' and I'm thinking wait a minute, I don't know if I want to be involved in this. Then Jay says, 'How do I know you?' And it turns out that her name was Celia Knight and she had spent some time with Nancy Hannum and had become friendly with Jonathan Sheppard. She was also a friend of Chris Collins, who was an amateur rider and a friend of Jay's. Chris was third in the National that Tommy Smith won and he is a fine guy. Anyway, Celia had gone back to England to live."

She also was Forster's friend and was helping him out with lunch. The four of them had a pleasant conversation, one thing leading to another, and it turned out that Knight's father owned a house, vacant at that time and only four miles away from Forster's yard. After lunch they all drove over and looked at the house, which appeared to be ideal for the Fenwick family. Things seemed to be falling into place.

For Captain Forster, it was a worthwhile risk to take on Ben Nevis. Although he had some good horses in training, he reasoned that he could use the attention that the British press would most certainly accord an American horse and jockey in order to attract more good horses.

Charlie was thinking, meanwhile, that because Forster did not have any big-name horses, chances were that with him the Americans would likely be big fish in a smallish pond. That was fundamentally important to Charlie because he wanted Ben Nevis to be the focal point in the yard. He wanted to get plenty of attention because he knew that he and his horse would need it to have a chance at winning the National. On that first summer's day, the talk between Charlie and Captain Forster was satisfactory on both sides.

Charlie went on to visit other trainers in other parts of the country, but with everything considered, Tim Forster seemed to have the most to offer. "So I selected Forster and it was probably the best decision I could have made," Charlie says. "There were reasons why it turned out so well that we didn't even consider at the time. Tim had wonderful facilities and they were all his own. Where Fred Winter was at Lambourn, there was no privacy; you were sharing with everyone. The gallops were everyone's gallops. It wasn't until later that I realized how important privacy was. And the village of Letcombe Bassett where the stables were was a great location. We could go into London for dinner or the theater and take the train and be home within an hour and 40 minutes. We were near the airport, and there were good schools right nearby, which Beth and Charlie attended. It just seemed like there were really an awful lot of good things that worked out for us."

Another great advantage that did not become apparent until later was that Graham Thorner rode for Forster. Thorner was a professional jockey who had been with Forster since leaving school in 1964. It was he who had ridden Well To Do when Forster won the 1972 Grand National. After racing and working with Forster for 15 years, Thorner's practical advice was to become invaluable for the Fenwicks, and his warm friendship irreplaceable.

Before Charlie left England in June 1978, he and Forster shook hands on the agreement to have Ben Nevis join the stables in Letcombe Bassett. From then on, things moved very quickly. While Ann stayed to arrange details at home, Charlie flew back over with Ben Nevis in the latter part of July. They left the Stewarts' stables on a hot morning and drove to Kennedy Airport outside New York City.

"Ben was held in a hanger with dozens of monkeys waiting to be shipped somewhere, and the smell and the noise were just unbelievable," Charlie recounts. "And I had to stay in a Westin hotel that was full of mobsters, and I remember thinking my life was just a dishrag that could be wiped out. I couldn't wait to get out of there."

Ben Nevis, on the other hand, remained untroubled by the monkeys and the subsequent flight to London, via Frankfurt, the next day. They flew on a 747 cargo plane with a specially constructed stall inside the hold. Charlie remembers that Ben Nevis was so calm that Charlie actually woke him up every time he went to check on him.

The morning after they arrived, Charlie met Forster at the stables. While one groom led Ben Nevis out of his stall, the other grooms (known as "lads" in the British Isles) gathered to see the American horse. Charlie wanted to caution them about Ben Nevis's idiosyncrasies. He said, "Now you've got to watch this horse. He's tough; he'll try to dump his rider."

He said that he had better just show them a few things they might need to know about handling the horse. The lads looked at one another, and Charlie could imagine them thinking, "Dumb Yank, what does he know about horses?" Charlie ignored the reaction and began to lunge Ben Nevis. Meanwhile, Forster went inside and got a camera to, as he said somewhat tongue-in-cheek, "take some pictures just in case he turns out to be a good one." A bit nettled, Charlie informed Forster that he was under the impression that the horse had already proved himself to be a good one.

Forster took one photo and then gave Charlie a leg up, and the minute Charlie got on Ben Nevis's back, the horse began his usual extravagant routine, giving an imitation of a rodeo horse fitted with a bucking strap. As Charlie remembers, "For about 30 seconds he walked around on his hind legs. Captain Forster stood there watching with his mouth open. Finally, when I dismounted, I

The first – and only – photograph Tim Forster took on the first morning.

asked him if he had gotten some good pictures. He shook his head, embarrassed. 'You know,' he answered, 'I was so intrigued by that performance that I forgot all about the camera.'"

Neither the horse's behavior nor his looks impressed the English trainer favorably. "When I first saw Ben Nevis," Forster recalls, "I looked at my head man and he looked at me and I said, 'He'll never get over three fences.'"

Fortunately unaware of the Englishmen's pessimism, Charlie settled in Ben Nevis to his satisfaction. Once the horse was taken care of, he saw to his family's arrangements, finalizing an agreement to rent the Knights' house and making plans for the children's education.

During the first week, Charlie stayed in a hotel, one evening dining at an Indian restaurant located around the corner. He ordered something and, not being very particular about his food, ate what was presented, even though it was not very good. By four o'clock that morning he was regretting it bitterly, becoming terribly sick. Morning finally came and Charlie struggled over to Forster's yard and got Ben Nevis tacked up, having to stop and rest on a bale of straw halfway through. Just then the head lad came by and saw him slumped and holding his head, prompting the lad to harrumph, "Too much London, I see."

Previously, Charlie had been advised by an American friend who had worked as a jockey in England that "you can do anything you want as long as you are there to ride out with that first lot every morning. If you do that, you will be okay, otherwise. . ." With that warning in mind, Charlie made it through the morning.

That same afternoon he had an appointment with a doctor for a physical examination, required for his license to ride in England. Although he still wasn't feeling much better, he kept the appointment. There were a number of people in the waiting room, but the receptionist took a look at Charlie, pale and sweating, and said, "You're really sick, aren't you?"

"Yes, I am," Charlie answered. She agreed to get him in to see the doctor right away. He went into an examination room and the doctor came in and asked him what he was there for. Charlie explained about the license, all the while wondering if he was going to be sick again. After the usual pulse and heart-rate tests, the doctor concluded cheerily that Charlie was in fine health and had passed the examination. Surprised and relieved but still feeling sick, Charlie didn't think that was the right moment to ask, "Great, and now while I'm in here, I really feel like hell. Can you give me something?"

Chapter Nine

On November 1, 1979, after the end of the American timber racing season, the Fenwick family, with nanny Rita Goolsby in tow, made the move to England. They had made arrangements for their horses and their household with help from their family and friends. Stewart was a generous supporter of the venture and had great faith in both Charlie and Ben Nevis. In fact, once the initial difficult period of trying to tame Ben Nevis was over, Stewart had not questioned the decisions Charlie and Ann made for the horse. He was as eager as they were about the coming adventure in England and enthusiastically backed their plans.

It did not take long for them to adjust to life in the small village of Letcombe Bassett. Although Goolsby has tales of constantly being cold and damp, of not having enough hot water, and of too many trips on foot to an inadequate grocery store, the Fenwicks did not notice or care about such things. They were thrilled to be in England.

They soon settled into a routine. Every morning Charlie would get on Ben Nevis at about 7:30 and go out with the first lot of horses being exercised, finishing by about 9:00. After the children were settled, Ann usually would join Graham Thorner and Charlie for breakfast in Captain Forster's dining room. Then she would ride out with them on the second lot at about 10 o'clock. Although Forster would not be described as warm and forthcoming, those breakfasts were congenial and provided Charlie with valu-

Charlie and Ben Nevis in the village.

able time with both Forster and Thorner. It was then that plans were discussed and strategies set forth.

One of their first decisions was to choose races for Ben Nevis. He needed to run in certain races in order to be handicapped so that he wasn't automatically assigned top weight (168 pounds) in the Grand National. There was some confusion over the best course of action, because Charlie and Forster had conflicting understandings of the rules.

The situation was further complicated when it became apparent that the two men differed in their approach to the horse's training. Forster was accustomed to adapting a horse's racing schedule to the animal's fitness, the weather conditions, et cetera. If a horse was not ready to run in one race, then another race was chosen, even if that meant waiting for months. The Fenwicks, on the other hand, wished to make all decisions about Ben Nevis's training with one goal in mind: preparing for the Grand National. They had very little time in which to get him ready; therefore, regardless of whether conditions were good or not, they felt that they needed to run their horse. It was extremely unlikely that they would have a second opportunity to devote as much time and effort toward a campaign for the National, and even if they did, Ben Nevis was not a young horse. This might be his only chance. As a result, they felt an urgency not shared by the English trainer.

By late November, when Ben Nevis still had not been entered in a race, Charlie's frustration peaked. One morning at breakfast he decided that it was time to get through to Forster to provoke some action. Ann, Charlie, Thorner, and Forster were sitting around the breakfast table. All was tranquil. Thorner had the newspaper by his plate and was reading while he ate, with all of them conversing a bit. Then, into a pause, Charlie said, "Tim, I really think it is time we get the show on the road."

With that, Thorner, being the most familiar with Forster's temper, picked up his paper and held it in front of his face, saying to no one in particular, "This will be interesting." He proceeded to hide behind the paper for the duration of the ensuing lively conversation.

"I started to barrage Tim," Charlie explains, "and he kept saying the ground was too hard, and he wanted to continue to go slowly until we got better ground. But as far as Ann and I were concerned, the ground was perfect, and we just didn't have the luxury of waiting anyway. Tim's point made perfect sense, but we had an 11-year-old horse and a guy who had to go back to work, and we had to get on with it."

Charlie eventually wore down Forster until the trainer exclaimed bitterly, "Okay, fine! Go ahead, break him down. See if I care. Break him down!"

Fred Winter once described the relationship between trainer and jockey as "close, personal, and often hellish difficult." The differences between an American stable and an English one – in daily routines, hierarchies, and even vocabulary – were significant and at times led to tension. And yet Charlie and Forster were able to work together. Forster appreciated that Charlie was straightforward and honest. When Charlie had first approached him, Forster recalled that, "Charlie said that he did not want to interfere with me, but that he knew the horse well and hoped that I would listen to him."

Each man learned the other's ways, and their respect for each other helped them resolve their differences. This was made easier in large measure by Forster's growing understanding of and respect for Charlie's toughness and determination.

A person important to Ben Nevis's adjustment to the English stable was his lad, Paul Simpson. In the British Isles, jobs in a stable are not split up between grooms and hotwalkers and jockeys as they are in the U.S. Instead, horses in training are divided between lads who have complete responsibility for the care – and usually the exercising – of their allotted charges. As Thorner notes, "Every single lad in England wants to be a jockey."

Charlie felt lucky that Simpson was assigned to Ben Nevis because he thought the lad was the best in the yard. Simpson had a very quiet manner around the horse and clearly grew to love him.

Graham Thorner rounded out the group working with Ben Nevis, although his influence on the horse was through Charlie. Thorner recounts warmly that "it was obvious from the word go that we were going to become great friends."

The English jockey became Charlie's mentor as well. He knew the ins and outs of steeplechasing in England and generously gave Charlie the benefit of his experience. Thorner was familiar with the races, the courses, the competition, and the pitfalls. His advice saved Charlie from making some of the more obvious mistakes that would otherwise have been inevitable. He also offered his encouragement and provided support and an example.

At 30 years old, Charlie was an amateur suddenly thrown into a world of professionals in another country. The change and the ensuing demands on him were great. Thorner became Charlie's sounding board, and what likely would have been some lonely and anxious times were lightened by Thorner's understanding and humorous insight.

Forster watched the friendship develop, and it became tacitly understood that while Thorner prepared Charlie to ride, Forster would prepare Ben Nevis to run. They became a good team.

At last it was time to race. Ben Nevis was entered in the Kenton Handicap Chase on December 15 at the Devon & Exeter meet.

Forster chose that race, an ordinary one at a lesser track, in order to avoid publicity. Already, the press was interested in the American story, and Forster knew that the more attention Ben Nevis received, the more pressure would be felt. Without a handicap rating in place, the American horse had to carry the automatic top weight. The competition was considered to be average, but the field numbered 17, about three times as large as those to which Ben Nevis and Charlie were accustomed.

The going was good and the start fast. Immediately, Charlie felt that his horse did not seem comfortable over the fences, although they were in second place when they turned for home. He poured on the speed to catch the leader but, uncharacteristically, Ben Nevis made a mistake at the last fence and unseated Charlie. When interviewed about the race weeks later, Charlie said, "I thought that Ben had really turned a double somersault when I saw him lying beside me on the ground, but the flood of photographs I received (later) showed emphatically that I was unseated, with Ben Nevis being knocked over by a following front runner after I had departed." Neither horse not rider was hurt, but it was a disappointing beginning.

The next try was at Kempton on the day after Christmas, known as Boxing Day, an important public holiday in Great Britain. It was an especially big day for Charlie: His brother Peter, his father and stepmother, and Redmond Stewart had come over for Christmas. The group was there to watch Ben Nevis run in the King George VI Chase, a top race that receives much attention in English sporting news.

After the fall at Devon & Exeter, Ben Nevis had not schooled very well and was given time off until Christmas Eve. He still did not seem to be going very well; in fact, Charlie remembers thinking that his horse was jumping fences as though they were a wall of fire. Ben Nevis could not seem to get used to the different construction of the English fences, which were brush, rather than the solid post and rail with which he was familiar. There was no fluidity to his performance.

Despite the worry, spirits rose Christmas morning. "We had a school up on the downs, and it was the most beautiful morning, no wind and just crystal clear," Charlie recalls. "My father and stepmother, Betty, and Mr. Stewart came up and watched, and Ben seemed to do better." There was great anticipation and a festive atmosphere when the group went to Kempton the next day.

Sixteen horses were to run, three of which had won their last time out. Royal Mail, from New Zealand, and Royal Frolic, two horses Ben Nevis would face many times in the coming months, were entered. In addition, several of Britain's top professional jockeys were riding, including John Francome and Tommy Carmody. Graham Thorner told Charlie that he would be surprised at how competitive the race was.

"I tried to get it over to him in very simple terms what was likely to happen, but until you've been there you just don't know," Thorner recounts. "I told him to get ready, that he would have the shock of his life."

Thorner predicted that the pace would be fast and the turns tight; if Charlie weren't careful, he'd be edged out of it and be behind the field before he realized what was happening. Charlie thought he could handle it "but it sure turned out to be exactly what Graham had said, and I never really gave Ben a chance," he recalls. "I got shuffled back and shuffled back rather than staying up and fighting for position. It was not a good race at all."

Ben Nevis finished eighth, his performance described in the Form Book as "always behind." Thorner says, "As soon as the race was over, Charlie wanted to do it again. He knew what he'd done and he was so mad at himself."

"That was a pretty low spot," adds Charlie. "We had been disappointed about the fall in the first race and then this. It just wasn't happening. I think one of the biggest problems at that time was that I, for one, had built this horse up so big in my mind that he was invincible, and I just couldn't believe that he was getting beaten. He trained like a great horse on the downs against the best of Tim's other horses. He was never outworked, he always seemed fairly impressive to me, but then it just wasn't happening on the race course."

In hindsight, Tim Forster blamed himself for choosing that race: "I shouldn't have entered him there; it was too high class a race for both the jockey and the horse then, but Redmond Stewart and all these Americans were coming over for it, so we stepped it up a bit."

Adapting to racing in the U.K. was a formidable challenge. Individuals familiar with steeplechasing on both sides of the Atlantic have noted that there is a gulf between British and American jumping that is as big as the gulf between amateur and professional sports. A steeplechase jockey in the U.S. might ride in 15 races in a season, with fields rarely larger than six or seven. In the U.K., an amateur jockey rides in 150 to 200 races per season, and a professional in as many as 600. The top British jockeys travel all over the country day after day, sometimes riding in as many as six jumping races in one afternoon, with fields regularly as large as 20 or 30 horses.

It was a lot to ask for Charlie to step into that world and grow accustomed to it in a matter of weeks, and yet he expected that of himself. Thorner recalls a time in those early days when it was obvious that Charlie felt the full weight of the undertaking he had set for himself. He had uprooted his household, leaving his job and the security of home to bring his wife and children to another country. Once there, he was not getting results that justified his decision. But out of the uncertainty and doubt came the increasingly strong determination to show the world what he could do.

In order to gain experience, it was imperative that Charlie ride in as many races as possible. So the Fenwicks embarked on a search for horses – a search that proved extremely frustrating and generally fruitless but that also provided them with invaluable future lessons.

Soon after Charlie had arrived in England, Forster showed him a horse named Medoc that was for sale. Peter Thompson, an avid American race horse owner, had earlier expressed an interest in having an English horse that Charlie could ride. After some trans-Atlantic phone calls, the Fenwicks bought Medoc for Thompson. Unfortunately, the horse quickly began to have soundness problems. Although those problems were ultimately solved and the horse later turned out to be of value, the timing wasn't right for Charlie.

The next attempt to secure a horse was through an Englishman named James Weatherby, who had visited Maryland in 1978. He had been entertained during Hunt Cup weekend by Charlie's father and had told Charlie to call him when the Fenwicks reached

England. Charlie phoned Weatherby, who treated him to an elegant and congenial lunch in London. Soon after, Weatherby called Forster and said he knew of a horse that Charlie and Ann might want to lease. The horse's name was Hovis, a brand of British cookie – or "biscuit," as the English say.

They went up to see the horse and had a big Sunday lunch with Weatherby, whom Charlie describes as "a terribly colorful and amusing fellow. I remember it was like a sucker punch. We had one of those midday dinners where all you want to do by four o'clock in the afternoon is lie down on the rug and go to sleep. After way too much port and brandy, we decided that we would try with this horse, although he did not look like a race horse at all; he was a butterball. But we called Peter Thompson and talked to him, and he said he'd go ahead and get this horse on some kind of lease arrangement."

Hovis was taken to Forster's yard, where Charlie rode him every day, but regrettably, he remained true to his name, resembling a big fat biscuit. Eventually they decided that he was not going to get any fitter so they might as well race him. "I remember we didn't want to take the quarter sheet off until he was out in the paddock practically galloping out on the course because we were embarrassed to let anyone see how fat he was," Charlie says. "It was just awful. He ran three times and was a disgrace every time."

The disappointments were mitigated, however, by the fun and the sense of adventure Charlie and Ann shared. Many of their American friends visited, and they enjoyed wonderful times together. The Fenwicks also became friends with several people with whom they had frequent contact through horse racing, among them, ironically, Fred Winter and his wife, Di.

Fred Winter is something of a legend in the jump world, as well as a formidable presence. Nonetheless, the Fenwicks describe him as a lovely guy who, far from haughty, scrubbed the mud off Ann's shoes after a tour of his muddy stable yard. The two couples spent many pleasant evenings together.

Jay Griswold was a welcome guest but endured an unwelcome brush with Tim Forster's temper on one occasion. Forster's stable yard was designed so that the stalls were on three sides of a square, facing inward, with a paved area directly in front of them. Beyond that, in the center, was a beautiful lawn. This lawn was Forster's pride, and it was absolutely forbidden to walk on the grass. Unfortunately, Griswold didn't know that, and one morning he strolled through the yard and straight across the lawn. He would have gotten away with it, but there happened to be a light dusting of snow on the ground that morning. When Forster came out into the yard a few moments later, he found telltale footprints. The whole yard heard him demanding to know who had walked on the pristine plot, and, American or not, visitor or not, the rules of the yard were vigorously described to the surprised and abashed Griswold, much to the amused delight of the lads.

On January 11, 1979, Ben Nevis ran at Wincanton in the John Bull Chase, an important step to get him handicapped for the Grand National. When Forster met Charlie in the paddock to give him a leg up, the trainer, never one to get his or anyone else's hopes up, imparted the following advice to Charlie: "Just keep remounting. I don't care how many times you fall off. You see that mound over there?" he said, pointing to a hill in the distance. "I don't care if Ben runs up there. You go get him and finish the race."

Ben Nevis broke in front and set the pace over the first half of the course, appearing far more at home than in his two previous outings. However, at the open ditch on the back side the second time around, he made a mistake. It appeared that he still wasn't comfortable with the brush fences, attempting to jump over them instead of through them, thereby jumping more cautiously and losing time. Royal Mail and Royal Frolic passed him and finished first and second, respectively, with John Francome riding the third-place finisher, Ballyfin Lake. Ben Nevis wound up fourth, but he ran better than he had yet in England. The papers quoted Forster as saying, "I am absolutely thrilled and delighted."

Soon after that race, Jonathan Sheppard visited for a few days. One morning at Forster's for breakfast, they were all joined by Bill Pape, president of the NSHA, Michael O'Hehir, an Irish radio commentator who had been calling the Grand National for the BBC for some 30 years, and Charlie Colgan, executive secretary of the NSHA. All were in the area to keep up on the racing scene.

That afternoon the group went out to the races at Chepstow in Wales. But when foggy conditions forced the cancellation of racing, they decided to meet in London for dinner. The hilarity of the group increased as the evening went on, and they weren't ready to adjourn when the pubs closed. Someone had the bright idea of going to the bar at the Hilton Hotel, reasoning, as best as they were able at that point, that because it was an American place, it would still be open. They trooped in and headed straight for the bar, trying to look as though they belonged there. A waiter, undeceived, said, "The bar is only open to guests of the hotel and what is your room number please?"

Sheppard, without missing a beat, replied confidently, "Oh, yes, it is 1425." It might have worked, but the hotel only went up to the 11th floor. The waiter was not amused, and the group's departure was precipitous.

The Fenwicks continued to search for horses for Charlie to ride and found one on a trip to Ireland. He was named Chiltown and belonged to a fellow who lived in the middle of a bog. It was twilight when they first saw the horse, which was beautiful. But as Ann recalls, "You couldn't see his coat and you couldn't see his feet, and that is something we learned the hard way ~ you don't look at a horse at twilight. That is a very big risk."

Charlie puts it more bluntly: "We just got robbed. It would have been better if they had put a pistol to our heads and taken all our money. Most everyone in Ireland knew about it, too – word gets around real fast there. The vet was supposed to be our friend and he should have known. I'm sure if we looked at the horse now we wouldn't make the (same) mistake, but what the hell, it was all part of the educational process, and we did have an awful lot of fun over there." Although they ultimately raced Chiltown, he was never any good.

While in Ireland, they got together with old friends. One time they were the guests of Ben Griswold, and often they stayed with Mrs. Miles Valentine and Jill Fanning and went foxhunting. The Fenwicks also met Phoncie O'Brien, who had been a steeplechase jockey. He was not only a lot of fun but also turned out to be a big help. His brother, Vincent O'Brien, who died in 2009, is regarded as one of the finest trainers of all time. He had winners at the Grand National a record three times in a row before becoming a trainer on the flat.

Charlie recalls a particularly memorable conversation with Phoncie: "We were talking about Ben's tendency to jump so high over the fences. Phoncie said Vincent used to train his horses over the hurdles even though they were going to jump the big fences, just to get them to quicken, and he suggested that that approach might help Ben. It made sense to Ann and me, so I talked it over with Graham to figure out what was the right way to approach Forster. We knew Tim would say, 'What does Phoncie O'Brien know about it?' and throw out the idea. So one day at breakfast I led up to the subject of schooling over hurdles and Graham chimed in and pretty soon Tim was agreeing that it might not be a bad idea. We left him thinking that the idea had been thought up at his breakfast table." That was in January of 1979, and schooling over hurdles became part of Ben Nevis's training from then on.

On February 3, Charlie returned to Ireland and won the Knocksinna N.H. Flat race on Bright Highway owned by his broth-in-law George Strawbridge. It was Charlie's first win in the British Isles and provided a timely boost to his confidence, although Charlie disclaims credit for the victory.

"Bright Highway turned out to be a good horse, and I'm not sure my winning on him really said anything about me," he allows. "We had a false start at first, and when we broke the second time, I was in front, which wasn't part of the plan, but it just happened that way. The race started off slow, and I was alone in front and actually I wasn't sure it had been a clear start. The going was pretty deep, so you couldn't hear anything, and we were racing right at the grandstand with the sun coming at us. That being the case, you couldn't glance to one side or the other to see if there were any shadows to tell that there were other horses near.

"The first stretch was right in front of the stands, and I was too embarrassed to be so amateurish as to turn and look behind and have the whole stands see me do that, so I just kept on, wondering all the time if I was all alone out there. I was thinking how horrible it would be if I was cantering away by myself and there were 20 guys milling around the start laughing their heads off. I thought, 'Oh, God, they'll really get a kick out of this one.' But finally after we'd gone about a half a mile, the pace picked up and a horse loomed up alongside, and I tell you I was glad to see it!

"We flew back that night feeling really good. The next morning Forster was full of congratulations, saying, 'Bloody well done, winning your first race in the British Isles' and so on. Then we went out to school Hovis, and for some reason the bastard stops at the first hurdle and throws me through his ears over the hurdle right on the ground. Well, Forster laughed and laughed, saying, 'Oh look at this, big fancy American fresh off winning a great race in Ireland and he falls at the first fence when his horse refuses!'"

In mid-February, Ben Nevis ran in the Compton Chase at Newbury, finishing a respectable third. The race was won by Gaffer, with Royal Mail second, but this time Ben Nevis beat Royal Frolic, who was fifth.

"We led a good bit, and Ben seemed to jump well," Charlie explains, "but he just didn't run any quicker at the end. Still, we were pleased; there were some good horses in the race."

His performance stoked the attention of the press and the betting public. In its February 16 issue, the British magazine *Horse and Hound* reported: "The revelation last week was Ben Nevis. In front after five fences, he stayed there, jumping superbly, until the third from home – and then ran on doggedly to finish only

12 lengths behind Royal Mail. I doubt if we shall see many better Grand National 'trials' – especially when you remember that
this tough, agile, adaptable 11-year-old has twice jumped around
the huge, unbreakable timber fences of the Maryland Hunt Cup."
Other press coverage called him a "live Grand National contender"
for the first time.

That allowed Charlie and Ann to hold up their heads a bit
more, recovering from the first series of disappointing races. Prior
to this time, they had not felt accepted by many of the racing people
they had met and it had been a lonely feeling at times. At last, their
results seemed to justify their efforts, and they grew more comfortable with their English peers. It seemed to the Fenwicks that they
had broken through the reserve with which they had been treated.

That reserve was noticeably not present with the jockeys Charlie came to know. "They were some of the nicest guys I met in
England," he says, "a really good bunch of people – hospitable,
friendly, and encouraging. And yet I think the English steeplechase
jockey is the toughest man in the world. It is the toughest way to
make a living, working six days a week and riding maybe six different horses in a day, and it is always cold and often raining sheets.
They are the most professional men that I know of, of really any
vocation. It takes a lot of courage to lead that sort of life. They live
with a certain amount of fear every single day. That creates camaraderie and brings out the best in people and a certain empathy
for each other. The weighing room was always a fun place to be, a
lot of chatter and banter and sometimes yelling and screaming. It
was always a hub of activity, and it was kind of fun just being part
of that. You had a valet who was in charge of your saddle and silks

and kept your things straight, and you could never see how, but somehow everything always got done."

Ben Nevis raced again on March 3 at Hereford, his last race before the National. In a four-horse race, he was a strong second to Royal Frolic. It was a good race and built up the American team's confidence.When Charlie won a race in Ireland one week later, things finally seemed to be gelling. Ben Nevis had been doing better and better, and Charlie had been able to ride in several races on various horses. He kept fit by riding, running, and playing squash.

Both horse and rider were ready by the end of March. Charlie made the 153-pound assignment the handicappers gave the Americans for the Grand National, establishing Ben Nevis second in weights. Charlie felt confident, and, according to Graham Thorner, he had good reason to feel that way: "I always said the only time Charlie was on equal terms and maybe a few pounds in hand for our racing was when he lined up in the Grand National. The first reason was the pace and the jumping of the horses: Ben's jumping was so good that I said at the time if he ran in the Grand National 10 times, he would win five times. The second reason was that it is more important to be a horseman than a jockey in the Grand National. And Charlie's asset was his horsemanship."

Chapter Ten

The Grand National steeplechase is conducted on 270 acres of land in Aintree outside of Liverpool. Since the race's inception in 1839, it has attracted an extraordinary amount of interest. Approximately 50,000 persons attended the first running. The big race on Saturday afternoon at 3:15 is the culmination of a three day meet with many races held every day. For some, the National becomes an obsession. The Duque de Alburqueque, a Spanish nobleman, saw a film of the race on his eighth birthday in 1926 and announced then that he would win the race someday. On his first try, he fell, cracking two vertebrae. The next year he fell again and was bruised badly. The third time he entered the race, he broke his leg; he had to pull up in his fourth attempt and broke his stirrup in his fifth.

In 1974, he entered the race yet again, although he had a broken collar bone at the time and had had 16 screws removed from one of his legs two weeks before the race. He still finished eighth. The Duque wanted to compete the next year, despite having broken a leg again one week before the race, and it was only when Fred Winter, his trainer, pointed out that it wouldn't be fair to the horse that he withdrew.

His seventh try was in 1976. On that occasion, he had a terrible fall at the 13th fence and was trampled by a succession of horses. He did not regain consciousness for two days, and his injuries included seven broken ribs, broken vertebrae, a broken wrist, a fractured right thigh bone, and a banged-up head. Unbelievably, he wanted to race the following year, but the Jockey Club, afraid for his life, introduced a rule that effectively barred him from competing; it stipulated that all jockeys more than 50 years old had to pass a medical examination. The Duque finally had to abandon his dream.

Many people have admitted to a passion to win at Aintree, among them Dick Francis, the champion jockey and popular mystery author, who once wrote, "Every steeplechase jockey has two ambitions. One is to ride more winners than anyone else in one season and become champion jockey for that year. The other is to win the Grand National at Aintree . . . In all my life I have never experienced a greater joy than the knowledge that I was about to win the National." That victory was snatched from him in a bizarre and heartbreaking calamity. His horse, Devon Loch, owned by the Queen Mother, was leading when he suddenly lost control of his legs and did a split, just yards from the finish line. He was unable to finish the race.

Perhaps no one has expressed his joy in winning the Grand National as unabashedly as Noel le Mare, who, late in his life, owned Red Rum. On the first of the three occasions that Red Rum won at Aintree, he said, "I have had three aims ever since I was a young man: to marry a beautiful girl, to become a millionaire, and to win the Grand National. Now I have achieved them all and it has made my life."

The power of the race to provoke strong emotions has been explained in many ways. John Hughes, who became clerk of the course in 1975, said, "The National really gets to you like no other race – not even the Derby with all its magic compares, and I was

10 years at Epsom. . . the incredible bravery of horse and rider sets the National apart." Hughes went on to say that the race's aura also includes "the charisma, the fun, and the camaraderie, like the night before the 1979 National when I happened to stay in the same small hotel as Charlie Fenwick and his friends."

Peter Bromley, a BBC racing correspondent since 1959, speculated once that the "fear of danger, I suppose, is what lifts it out of the ordinary. I really do feel quite frightened for the competitors when they are lining up before the race. I think that any moment now one of them could be coming back on a stretcher. Aintree is an amazing course, an astonishing arena for great events to happen."

Many extraordinary stories surround the Grand National. In 1871, Lord Poulet, who owned a horse called The Lamb, had two dreams before the race: In one, his horse was first; in the other, last. He wrote to the jockey that he had seen in the dream of victory, explained his vision, and asked him to ride; the jockey agreed and they won the race. One year's winner, Grudon, negotiated the course in a blinding snowstorm with two pounds of butter stuffed into his hooves to prevent the snow from balling. In 1904, the New Zealand horse Moifaa was shipwrecked off the Irish coast on his way to England to race. He swam ashore to safety and won the National that same year.

Some winners seemed unlikely prospects. Teal, who won in 1952, was once offered – and rejected – for sale at two pounds, 10 shillings. Another pulled a cart for the landlord of a pub for three years before his victory. Red Rum, the only horse to win the Grand National three times, was humbly stabled behind a car showroom and taken through the streets to train on a nearby beach.

There have been as many as 66 entries and as few as 10. The Grand National has seen its share of tragedies, with jockeys and horses losing their lives taking part in the race. Several times one or two riderless horses have turned the race into a shambles, often causing serious injury. In one telling of the 1928 race, the favorite refused the ditch in front of the Canal Turn fence, ruining the chances of 20 other runners; in another version, a horse became stuck atop of that fence and put 35 horses out. Downey Bonsal, Redmond Stewart Jr.'s first cousin, rode Burgoright, a 1925 Maryland Hunt Cup winner, in the 1928 Grand National. Unfortunately, he was one of the ones brought down in the confusion. The race was finally won by 100-1 shot Tipperary Tim. The second-place – and only other – finisher was Billy Barton, who belonged to Howard Bruce, Charlie's grandfather.

In 1967, the calamity was even more remarkable. As the field approached the 23rd fence, two loose horses suddenly began running up and down in front of it. Havoc reigned as horses helplessly fell over one another, with only one runner escaping the melee. That was Foinavon, again a 100-1 shot, who was so far behind that his jockey, John Buckingham, had time to size up the situation. He came out of nowhere, picking his way through the tangle and over the fence. He then cantered home to uncontested victory and general astonishment.

The course is almost two and a half miles around; the horses make two circuits, for a total distance of about four and a half miles. It has 30 fences. Much has been written about the fearsome jumps, but even if a horse negotiates all of them successfully, there is still a 494-yard run-in to the finish. It can seem like an eternity for fatigued horses and riders.

Many second-place finishers would have given much to have had the course just a few yards shorter. Richard Pitman, a top National Hunt jockey turned racing commentator, is one of those. He was caught and passed by Red Rum two strides from the finish. "The run-in between the last fence and the line was the most agonizing 494 yards that I will ever travel," Pitman once wrote. "My aching limbs had now given their best, and every breath I snatched scalded my windpipe as if it was boiling water. I'd never known tiredness like it before. Each jump takes something out of you and you feel your strength going from your fingers to start with, they begin to go a bit rubbery, and then your wrist and then right up your forearm. You have exhausted your physical depths. . ."

Each year for weeks before the meeting at Aintree, the English newspapers are full of stories about the Grand National, with past and potential winners described for an eager public. Charlie and Ben Nevis attracted considerable attention, and Charlie was the subject of several interviews. Richard Pitman recalls, "We followed him for the BBC. We made him the object of two of our specials, because we really did think he had a major chance."

There were headlines such as "Battling Ben," "A Yankee Tackles Aintree," "Charlie Takes Chance on Ben," and "What a U.S. Roar if Ben Nevis Triumphs!" Articles pointed out Ben Nevis's U.S. record and his continually improving performances in Britain. *The Daily Telegraph* reported: "Apparently pretty slow when he first came back to this country, Ben Nevis has been steadily acclimatizing ever since and adjusting his jumping from the rather over-cautious method demanded by the solid timber of Maryland. His form has improved correspondingly and last time out at Hereford he finished at level weights alongside Royal Frolic, who has to give him 8 lbs. at Aintree."

While it felt good to read the positive press, the pressure on the Fenwicks began to mount accordingly. Tim Forster had another horse, Mr. Snowman, entered in the race, with Graham Thorner as his rider. That increased the attention focused on the yard. Charlie and Thorner talked at length about the race, and Charlie worked out his strategy according to the experienced jockey's practical advice.

Charlie remembers gratefully that "there were some basic things he told me about, like, you jump the first six fences straight in a row. The third fence is an open ditch and the last of the sequence is Becher's Brook. Those first fences can get repetitious, and you can't see which fence you're on because each looms up like a wall in front of you. You can lose track of how many fences you've jumped. Graham said that as you come to Becher's there is a hedge on the left hand side that comes out from the fence probably 100 yards, and he said, 'Don't forget when you see the hedge it's Becher's Brook,' and that was pretty important, because if you didn't know it was Becher's, you'd have a nasty shock. There is one more fence and then the Canal Turn, after which you turn sharply to the left. Graham said that it is good to be on the inside there because then you are in good position to go to the next fence. Everyone bunches up and you just have to wait your turn. That turned out to be right, and it wasn't as chaotic as it looked if you did wait your turn. There were a lot of things like that that Graham told me which turned out to be helpful."

A large group of friends and family from Maryland began to arrive in England. Many had been asked to place bets on Ben Nevis for others who stayed home. One friend, John "Johnny" K. Shaw III, had about $2,000 to bet, and another, Nathaniel "Nat" S. Prentice, had several hundred dollars. Prentice remembers that for a couple of days before he left Baltimore, he was stopped in the street by friends pulling loose cash out of their pockets and thrusting it upon him to bet for them.

Charlie and Ann drove up to Liverpool on Friday morning, March 30, with Ann's father, Charlie's brothers Bruce and Ned, and his father and stepmother. They went out to walk the course in the afternoon with Thorner, and were joined by more and more people until there was a group of about 50 following them. Janet Auchincloss, mother of Jackie Onassis, was among them, and she asked Charlie if it was alright if she called him by his first name. He replied that she should go right ahead, he didn't mind at all.

When they reached the fence known as the Chair, she said something like, "My God, what is this?" Thorner didn't know and didn't care who she was. To him she was just another silly American betraying her ignorance of what is practically a British landmark, so he responded disgustedly, "That's the Chair, lady," and turned away pointedly, much to Charlie's amusement.

The fences are constructed of blackthorn trees covered with layers of green spruce branches. Although the horses are able to brush through the top eight to 10 inches, the fences are solid enough for a man to stand on. Trouble often comes from the hazards on either side: the wide ditches in front and the steep drops on the landing side. The third fence, for example, has a ditch six feet wide and three feet, six inches deep in front. Becher's Brook, the sixth fence, is dreaded because of a sheer drop of 12 feet from its top to the mud and water of the brook behind it. There is a

Tommy Smith standing on top of Becher's Brook before his race on Jay Trump in 1965.

sharp grade up from the brook, so a horse has no leverage to keep from tipping over if he fails to jump clear. Also, because of the thick fences and drops, it is impossible to see from the take-off side what lies, sometimes literally, on the landing side.

Bruce Fenwick was among the group that toured the course before the race. "When I saw those fences," he explains, "I remember thinking that if every horse fell down, it wouldn't surprise me. I was sick to my stomach when I walked that course."

Chapter Eleven

The tension and excitement continued to build throughout the day and night before the race. The American group was in high spirits. Many of them were staying at Liverpool's Adelphi Hotel, headquarters for the majority of owners, trainers, riders, and foreign spectators. The Adelphi is famous for being the scene of much Grand National revelry. People do, with some regularity, swing on its chandeliers and take shelter from flying debris under the piano. Charlie and Ann and another group of friends were staying at a smaller hotel, where they too had a lively evening.

By 7:00 a.m. the next morning when Charlie arrived to walk the course again, the crowd that would total 66,000 by race time had begun to gather. The weather was perfect. For the Grand National, spectators arrive by train, plane, car, and chartered bus, spreading out over the stands and around the course. Thousands choose to watch from the railroad embankment at the side of the course. Racegoers dress in everything from caps to feathered hats, suits to jeans, silk to leather. They come with picnics and binoculars and walking sticks and high hopes for their favorite horse. A good sprinkling of major and minor European royalty is always on hand.

"There was so much going on that I didn't have time to think too much. It was all so new to me," Charlie says. "But as (race) time got closer, Ann and I began to get nervous. I was glad to go over to the jockeys' room and spend the afternoon there. That was great. There was a lot of talk and camaraderie and a television so we could watch the other races going on.

"Just before the race, Lord Derby, a senior member of the Jockey Club, came in to give his talk, which he gives every year. It's the tradition, and he always says the same thing, somewhat avuncular and ponderous: 'Now boys, there are four and a half miles to go and big fences and just don't go too fast. . . particularly down to the first fence.' And you get a lot of smart remarks in the background: 'Right, Lord Derby, you try to ride the bugger I'm on' and that sort of thing. No one pays any attention, and you're sort of embarrassed that people are as rude to him as they are. But he seems oblivious to it fortunately. Then they call us out and there are more than 30 different outfits in the paddock, and it's hard to find your group. I sort of wandered around for a while until I found Ann and Tim."

Nat Prentice describes the occasion this way: "We were able to get in on the paddock scene, and I recall Ann and her sister looking very grand. I don't know, maybe they rented some furs or something, but they looked like they belonged there with the Aga Khan. Ann was in her pre-race mode of concentrating so hard on what was happening that she didn't have room to do anything but acknowledge us with sort of a Queen Mum wave. Then we went up on the roof to watch."

Nat's wife, Anita, adds, "It was very crowded up there, but what a beautiful day! There was a luminous blue sky and scudding clouds, and there were all of those riders in silks streaming out in a parade with their colors vivid against the green grass. It was full of pageantry and a captivating sight."

Paul Simpson held Ben Nevis while Tim Forster gave Charlie a leg up. The paddock was jammed with people and horses, and Simpson had his hands full trying to avoid being trampled as Ben Nevis became agitated. Then the field of 34 paraded onto the course. Charlie remembers, "Ben hated the whole idea of walking down and back in front of the stands. He wasn't settled, he was jigging around, anything but relaxed."

Finally, it was time to line up. Riders jostled each other for their favored positions and suddenly were in line. Final odds flashed on the board, with Ben Nevis held at 15-2. The tape went up. They were off.

One of Charlie's first impressions was "how eerie it was to see a horse and rider go over a fence in front of you and not reappear. Because of the size and construction of the fences, you'd have no idea where they might be when you came over, so there was no way to avoid them before you were literally on top of them. I was definitely aware of the drop on the landing side, but Ben handled that part of it very well. There were falls all around us. There was an Irish jockey who broke his shoulder at the first jump, and I think his injuries can be attributed to us. He came off right into our path.

"And another thing I'll always remember is the noises! I noticed it several times. I could hear loud snapping sounds like bones cracking when those falls were happening. I know bones weren't being broken, but still, when those horses were falling, I could hear that crunch and it sounded awful."

Charlie also recalls riding near John Francome, who was aboard eventual third-place finisher Rough and Tumble. Francome was full of chatter. "I think he might have been talking to Graham," Charlie notes. "He was so casual he sounded like he was out for a ride for fun on an afternoon in January."

Going to the start.

Ben Nevis was jumping smoothly, and, with his usual cleverness, staying out of trouble; at two fences he sidestepped fallen horses. Once over the 14th fence, he and Charlie had almost completed the first circuit. The Chair was next. From some yards out, that fence develops into a sort of a funnel, and at that time there was no way for a riderless horse to get off the course. When Charlie and Ben Nevis approached the Chair, two loose horses were zigzagging back and forth to avoid having to jump the fence. First the riderless horses went left, then high up on the right. Still searching for an escape route, they wound up directly in front of the fence and in the path of oncoming horses, nine of which were brought down as a result.

Spectators could see the disaster developing. As Prentice tells it, "To be honest, the only part of the race we really saw well was

Charlie's fall. He couldn't have done it in a better place, because we all could see it. If he had fallen on the back side, we just would have heard, 'Fenwick down,' and we would have been worried about his health. But we saw him get up. We could see what was going to happen; we saw the loose horses cut right in front and then balk at the jump. The leading horses had to try to jump the loose horses; you could see it unfold, and there was nothing Charlie could do. It was a crushing disappointment."

Bruce Fenwick recalls, "It was like the Civil War movies where horses are falling down all over the place. Charlie was knocked sideways."

"I saw them coming," Charlie says, "and I tried to get another stride. I tried my best to get another stride."

Ben Nevis courageously tried to jump clear but was hampered by one of the loose horses. He landed on top of the fence and then kicked clear, throwing Charlie off in the process. Charlie immediately sprang to his feet, caught the horse, and remounted; he jumped the next fence but then, realizing that it was fruitless and that he was exposing himself and the horse to pointless injury, he pulled up, then turned and walked off the course.

"It was tough," Charlie admits. "I don't think I have ever experienced anything as frustrating in my whole life. Everything that we had done for such a long period of time was all wrapped up in one little span of time and then it was all poofed away. It was crushing."

There was not much for anyone to say. The Fenwicks had come 6,000 miles and anticipated the race for nearly 12 months. In all of that time, almost every decision in their lives was made with the Grand National in mind. There was a tremendous sense

Ben Nevis falling at the Chair in the middle of the photo.

of anticlimax and emptiness. Of the nine horses that had been brought down in the debacle at the Chair, tragically, two died. One was Alverton, the race-time favorite. His jockey, Jonjo O'Neill, was unhurt, but, kneeling beside his dead horse, he wept. Graham

Thorner fell at the 22nd fence, remounted, and then pulled up at the 27th. Rubstic, a Scottish horse, eventually won.

That night Redmond Stewart gave a party at the Adelphi Hotel for the American contingent. It was a relatively quiet affair, and the group split up the following day. The next night, Charlie and Ann hosted a party to say thank you to their English friends. Ben Nevis was back in his own stall by then, looked after by Paul Simpson. The plan all along was to run him in France in early summer in the Grand Steeplechase de Paris, and so Ben Nevis stayed in Captain Forster's yard. On Monday morning the Fenwick family flew home.

Chapter Twelve

The Fenwicks settled back into their lives in Maryland. Their children went to school to finish spring term, and Charlie began to work with his father in the automobile business. Their horses returned to the Stewarts' stables, and Charlie and Ann resumed training. Timber racing season was just peaking, and they immediately threw themselves into its midst. Charlie rode Dosdi in the Maryland Grand National three weeks after his return and won the race. One week later, Charlie and Dosdi won the Hunt Cup, too.

"Charlie came back from England and tore the U.S. apart," Paddy Neilson says. "He won everything in sight. But his mood was tail-between-his-legs, and he said, 'Boy, I thought we knew a whole lot and we don't.' He always wants to win; I guess anything less is a failure to him. But you know, the whole time Charlie and Ann were in England, they were sopping everything up, and there is just so much you can sop up all at once. And they never got any breaks actually racing Ben over there; the luck went against them all the time as far as the weather and the competition and the way the races developed.

"I think Charlie is a wonderful jockey, the best timber rider I have ever seen. Before he went to England, he was still a little rough from a style standpoint. He always had a very good eye and presented a horse to the fence very well, but he didn't look very good. He learned a lot from watching the English professionals, and when he came back he was a polished rider."

Turney McKnight had similar impressions: "I did notice a difference in Charlie when he came back. Which again says something for Charlie, because some people go over there and never see anything. He came back with an acute awareness of how fit those jockeys are, how tough they are, and how competitive it is. He came back with a new sense of style – I think an English rider rides with a straight low back and their position never changes even during the jump. I think it is easier to present a horse to a fence in a relaxed and balanced way from that position than from standing up straight. When Charlie came back, he rode more like the English jockeys, and I believe that made a difference to his success. He had developed an awe and respect for the English steeplechase jockey, and I think he looked on the year over there not as a negative thing but a positive thing, a learning experience. I think he was excited by it."

The race in France was coming up. Charlie could not make the weight of 140 pounds, so Graham Thorner would ride Ben Nevis. The Grand Steeplechase de Paris in Auteuil is France's major steeplechase. Jay Trump had entered the race after his win in the English Grand National, and it seemed to make sense to give Ben Nevis a try at it. Ann went over in late May to join Thorner at the training center in Chantilly. She recalls with amusement, "The French people couldn't understand it; here was this young couple over there, and they would have every meal together and talk and laugh companionably, but then they would go upstairs to different bedrooms every night. The French would shake their heads: 'Foreigners!' they'd say."

It was not a successful trip from a racing standpoint, but it did have its funny moments. The first morning there, Thorner told the

French trainer that he wanted to tack up the horse his way, with English girths. The suggestion was not well received. A jockey, even worse an English jockey, does not tell a French trainer what to do, and the Frenchman insisted that he would do it his way. When the trainer leaned in to tighten the girths, Ben Nevis reacted predictably to anyone who knew him - that is, by rearing back and prancing on his hind legs. The trainer was stunned and quickly called for English girths, while Ann and Graham tried to hide their laughter.

Ben Nevis needed a preparatory race before the big one, so he was entered in the Prix Millionaire II at Auteuil on May 28. In a 16-horse field, he ran well but tired in the latter stages to finish 11th. He was not quite fit, and he definitely was not comfortable over the fences, which were constructed differently from those in both England and America. Graham and Ann talked to Charlie, and, collectively, they decided that it wasn't worthwhile to pursue Ben Nevis's training in France, asking him, in effect, to learn another style of jumping. So they cancelled their plans for the Grand Steeplechase.

As Tim Forster remembered it," As far as I knew, that was going to be it. Ben Nevis was going to go home after France. Everyone had tried their best, but that was that. Then Ann rang me up to say they were going to give the National another try, and I was very pleased."

Ann and Graham had conferred with Charlie and Redmond Stewart over the telephone and the group had decided to give Ben Nevis one more chance at Aintree.

Kathy Ingalls, Ann's sister, says, "Not one of us who went over there to see the race in '79 thought Ben Nevis would have a shot at winning it another year. But Dad was so generous and such a sportsman. He said to Charlie that he would pay the bills and Charlie should go back and ride Ben Nevis again."

To anyone not intimately familiar with the situation, it was a surprising decision. The facts were that Ben Nevis had not won one race in England and had just failed in France. However, Charlie felt that he knew his horse, knew his capabilities. The race at Aintree had been Ben Nevis's best since leaving the U.S., and he had been going strong when he was brought down. Charlie was convinced that Ben Nevis could win the Grand National. That compelling belief overrode the inevitable difficulties in making a second attempt. The Fenwicks were fortunate to have Stewart's support in what looked like a quixotic quest.

The greatest obstacle to overcome was the distance between Charlie's home and the horse. The Fenwicks had agreed that it was impractical and undesirable to move the whole family to England again. Therefore, Charlie would have to commute to England to ride Ben Nevis in races.

Beginning in November, after a very successful fall season at home, Charlie began making trips to England. Flying on stand-by flights and often staying only three or four days, he made seven trips and raced 10 times in five months. On four of those occasions he rode Ben Nevis; his other mounts were Whistle for Gold, Chiltown, and Medoc.

Ben Nevis's first race was at Lingfield, where he finished second in spite of carrying a lot of weight, an encouraging start. In many ways, this second English campaign was easier. Ben Nevis and Charlie had become familiar with the conditions and they made fewer mistakes. Also, as Forster asserted forcefully, "The pressure was off. No one paid any attention. Ben was a perfectly normal horse, and there wasn't any big deal. Not like the first year when every time Charlie rode, the press would cover it and hordes of Americans would come over to watch. That had put on so much pressure."

Still, the second year wasn't without its disappointments. Ann and Charlie went over for a week at the end of November, and, on the 29th, Ben Nevis ran at Haydock. The race was four miles long, and Ben Nevis finished sixth. Charlie was not pleased with his own performance, feeling that he had not ridden well enough to give Ben Nevis a good chance. The day after Haydock, the Fenwicks ran Medoc at Leicester. He finished fifth, and the couple flew home somewhat dispirited.

The next trip was more encouraging. In December, Charlie and his father flew to England together. After they landed, they drove straight to Chepstow where Charlie rode Chiltown in a race. The next day he rode Ben Nevis in the Manns Handicap Chase at Warwick. One paper reported that Ben Nevis "failed by only half a length to concede 10 pounds to Peter Scot. Charlie Fenwick, now a regular and most welcome visitor to our shores, was clearly well pleased with the performance of his father-in-law's (horse), and said, 'That is the best race he has run in this country.' Sent to the front at the start, Ben Nevis still held the advantage at the last, where Peter Scot was brought to challenge, the latter getting away from the fence the quicker to clinch the issue."

After Christmas, Charlie made a fruitless trip to England with his mother. Although he rode Chiltown in a novice chase, the weather was so miserable that they couldn't get in a race for

Ben Nevis. "Mother and I kicked around and looked at castles but finally we had to give up and come home," Charlie recalls.

He was unable to make another trip very soon, so Hywel Davies, an English jockey, rode Ben Nevis at Sandown on January 4. With three fences left, they were just behind the leader, but weakened late; two horses passed them, leaving Ben Nevis to finish fourth.

Graham Thorner did not ride Ben Nevis because he had retired several months earlier. However, unknown to Tim Forster and several owners who begged Thorner to come out of retirement for a special race or horse, he and Charlie had made an agreement. Charlie had said to his friend one day, "What would happen if I got hurt? Who would ride Ben at Aintree?" Thorner replied that Ben Nevis was the only horse for which he would come out of retirement. All through that winter and early spring, he kept his license. The day after the Grand National, he handed it in.

In February, Ben Nevis ran at Doncaster. Charlie had been struggling to make the weight for the race, even resorting to trying to sweat it off. He was staying alone and had a long miserable drive to get to the course. When the race went off, it was 36 degrees and raining. The day was a write-off, with Ben Nevis finishing 32 lengths behind the winner.

The following day, though, Charlie rode Medoc at Huntington for Peter Thompson. "It was a novice chase," he remembers, "which by definition is a hairy event. There were riders getting thrown off, but it was a lot of fun. In a small way, (I felt that) it was a privilege to be riding with the pros, and it was fun." He finished third and was pleased with the result.

Point-to-point racing in Maryland began in March. During the week before the English Grand National, Charlie had two winners riding for his brother Bruce. It was good to have the races to help him get fit, but one of the horses, Snowy Dawn, pulled to the left and Charlie's right arm was terribly sore afterward. He couldn't even lift his arm to put on shaving cream. Nonetheless, the back-to-back victories built his confidence, and his arm had healed by the time he returned to England.

The build-up to the Grand National was very different this time. Ben Nevis received scant attention from the British press. The brief mentions he did get were along the lines of the following in *The Sporting Life*; "The American-owned and ridden Ben Nevis was one of the Chair casualties last year. He has yet to win a race in England, was beaten a long way when last of three finishers at Doncaster on his most recent run, and was many lengths behind Jer and Salkeld at Haydock in November." (Jer and Salkeld were to be contenders at Aintree.)

Ben Nevis did not attract the same interest at home, either. The general reaction was one of puzzlement at the Fenwicks' determination to try again. The prevailing attitude was that it was understandable to try once but excessively optimistic to go back a second time. Many had lost interest in Ben Nevis's progress and did not bet on him again. Dale Austin, a sportswriter for 30 years who saw countless athletes come and go, was not among the disbelievers. He said of Charlie, "I don't think I've ever seen anyone try so hard to win something. He made the last full measure of effort for his goal. By the nature of my work, I don't really root for any one person, but I couldn't help but root for Charlie on this one."

Some from Maryland who did bet – even if it was more in support of Charlie than in any real expectation of a payoff – again gave Johnny Shaw the job of placing their wagers in England. Once in London, Shaw bet at the same bookmaker's window where he had placed money the previous year. The bookmaker looked up when he heard the request and the accent, and said with broad smile, "Oi remember you! You're the bloke what paid for me 'olidays last year!" He gladly took the American money again, and Johnny Shaw still chuckles over that fact.

Chapter Thirteen

On Thursday, March 27, 1980, Charlie and Ann arrived in England with a few friends and family members. Sadly, Ann's mother was ill, so Redmond Stewart was unable to join them. They gathered first at Graham Thorner's house. Charlie played squash in the morning and the whole group spent the afternoon in front of the television watching racing, held in the pouring rain, at Aintree. That night, Wallace Lanahan, who had supported Charlie unfailingly through the years, gave a big dinner party in London at the Barclay Hotel.

"I was delighted that Charlie could join us," Lanahan says. "I didn't want to distract him from the main task at hand, but Charlie is a real goer. I gave a little toast and said we all looked forward to seeing him come down the stretch after the last fence with that big smile of his, looking back to see where the other horse was." Those words proved prophetic.

Ann admits that when she heard the toast, "Charlie and I were gagging a little at that point. We were not as optimistic. It had rained and rained and rained, and we were convinced that Ben couldn't run anywhere on soft ground. All of us were saying, 'Oh the rain!' But Wallace, he wasn't deterred at all. He just was sure we were going to win, period, no problem, over and out."

Ben Nevis had almost always run on hard ground, and he ran so well under those conditions that Charlie and Ann assumed he would not run well when the going was soft, hence their foreboding about the weather conditions.

On Friday afternoon the group drove up to Liverpool and went to see the racing at Aintree. "It was still raining like crazy," Charlie recalls. "I remember Ann and Jay Griswold and I standing under the grandstand watching a hurdle race, and it was raining as hard as you ever see it rain. You just felt like no more water could fit into the air. All of a sudden we started to get pushed forward. There was such a mob that if we hadn't moved, we would have been trampled, and we looked and saw that a hole had broken through the roof. All the water that was on the roof was pouring in through the hole – it was (like) a waterfall. You would have drowned if you had stood there. It cleared out the grandstand, so we had to stand out in the weather, and it could not have been more unpleasant. And of course the ground was diabolically deep. Everyone was having a fit. All we could think of was that Ben didn't like wet ground."

One concern that was lessened for the 1980 race was that the course had been altered as a result of the disaster at the Chair the year before. The fence had been modified so that there was an escape route for loose horses. (Due to the number of horses that have been injured or killed in the Grand National, the race's stewards have made the course less perilous in recent years.)

By the next morning, the storm had passed and the sun was out. Charlie says, "Ann and I went out to the course early. There was lots of action, all the early gossip. . . who was scratched and who had coughed the night before and so on."

Charlie did not know that Ben Nevis had been one of those coughing earlier in the week. Tim Forster's lads had heard him cough 15 times on Tuesday, and the trainer had been very concerned, but the cough had not persisted. Forster hadn't told the Fenwicks, not wanting to worry them needlessly.

Charlie jogged on the beach with Griswold, and then bought a puzzle of Red Rum for his children. He remembers saying to his friend, "If I owned Ben Nevis and lived in England and had other chances to do this, I wouldn't run Ben today." But although he was concerned about how the horse would handle the conditions, he himself was ready. He had gotten down to 152 pounds by playing squash and running and riding, the lightest he had been in 12 years.

The schedule was similar to that of the preceding year. Charlie and Ann walked the course with Graham Thorner in the morning, growing more nervous as the minutes passed. Prince Charles also walked the course, protected by knee-high Wellington boots. A photo of him on the course shows him ankle-deep in water, and the ground was being described as a gluepot by racing writers.

Thorner told Charlie that the ground had not been that soft since he himself had won the race in 1972, and that most of the jockeys would be unfamiliar with racing the course under those conditions. He said that the way to approach the race was to think of just "hunting" around on the first circuit and only to start to ride a race on the second circuit. He advised Charlie to creep through the field, taking things as they came. Finally, just before Charlie left for the jockeys' room, Thorner looked at him and said, "Make sure you get round this time. Not many will."

The jockeys' room was warm and cheerful, and Charlie was glad to join the other riders there. His valet that day was John Buckingham, the former jockey who had won the National in 1967 on Foinavon. Buckingham had also been valet for Thorner in 1972,

117

when Graham won on Well To Do. Charlie chose to see the coincidence as a good omen.

Lord Derby came in and gave the same speech, and everyone was just as rude. Then the jockeys were called out. Once again, Charlie had to wander around among the many groups in the paddock before he could find Ann and Tim Forster, with Paul Simpson holding Ben Nevis. There was little talk.

"I didn't give Charlie any instructions," Forster recalled. "In that race, a clear run is the most important thing, and, historically, people have won from every place - outside, inside, middle - and there is no point in discussing it. You just want to get on with it and get a clear run, and I knew Charlie could do that because he is a horseman."

Forster gave Charlie a leg up and Ben Nevis a final pat on the neck. Charlie turned and followed the line of riders.

"We went out and warmed up," Charlie says, "and once I was on the horse I was happy. Everything was pretty straightforward at the start. I just wanted to get off to a nice start, and we did. There was a fair bit of early pace, and I remember Ben was the last horse to land over Becher's Brook the first time, but he was jumping beautifully and everything was going well. He was in the back third of the field for the first circuit, and he was jumping terrifically. Unlike the previous year when things seemed to conspire against us, everything seemed to go our way. When horses fell, they fell away from us instead of in our path as before. Everything was straightforward until we got to the Chair, where again things funneled down. Everybody got jammed up, but Ben ended up jumping it, although he struggled to some degree to get over."

The early pace and the fatigue from pulling hooves out of the sodden turf soon began to take a toll. More and more horses simply could not get into the air over fences that were a couple of inches higher than usual because of the deep going. Rubstic, the 1979 winner who had never fallen in his career, made a mistake and went down at the Chair.

Charlie kept Ben Nevis on the inside, which cuts off some big corners, thereby getting into good position for the succeeding fences. Additionally, there is usually less traffic there because many jockeys do not like the inside; the drops on the landing side are considerably bigger. A jockey must have a lot of confidence in his mount to choose that strategy.

"By not doing anything in particular," Charlie continues, "when we started back out on the second circuit, Ben was right up there with the leaders because so many horses had fallen. In four fences we had gone from being virtually nowhere to being up front. We jumped the next six fences even with Delmoss, and we weren't racing – we were just galloping around. Ben's expertise was apparent then. I was on the outside when we jumped Becher's Brook the second time and Delmoss fell. That put Ben in the front by about 10 lengths, and that was the first time he had been well established in front in a race the whole time he had been in England. We turned and then jumped Valentine's Brook and we were right close to the rail on the inside.

"There is a macadam road that goes down inside the rail where the truck taking the film of the race drives. The noise of that truck made Ben pick up the bit because he thought the truck was chasing him. It was fortunate because we were in front by 10 lengths, and I think he would have lost interest and just cantered

Charlie with white cap coming over the Chair. John Francome on
Rough and Tumble is #8 and Rubstic is on the ground.

along otherwise. I really would have had to work on him to keep
him from giving up the lead that he had.

"We jumped the next four or five fences that way, with the
truck right beside him, and that really did us a lot of good. It takes
a lot of courage for a horse to jump that many fences so far in front,
and there just wasn't a whole lot of competition left in the race at
that point. From the time we jumped Becher's Brook and Delmoss
fell, we never heard from another horse. Rough and Tumble was
always clearly second."

In its account of the race, *The Maryland Horse* reported: "Two
horses bit the dust at the first and two more at the third, including
the heavily backed Jer. . . Becher's claimed So and So and Another

Dolly, whose rider, champion Jonjo O'Neill, has yet to complete the course.

"As the horses streamed over the Canal Turn and on towards Valentine's, Ben Nevis showed in the middle of the field, still some 20 lengths adrift of the leader Delmoss. . . At the Chair, Delmoss still led, with the dubious companionship of a loose horse beside him. A wall of horses lay a length behind with still more, including the improving Ben Nevis, close up. Rubstic, among the leading group at the time, hurtled through the top of it and paid the obvious penalty. Both Flashy Boy and The Vintner were halted in their tracks and Ben Nevis himself had to scramble over the fallen favorite.

"Out onto the second circuit, with 14 more fences still to take, several horses were tiring rapidly. Aintree hadn't known such heavy going in living memory and the normally springy turf was now more like a sodden sponge. One still full of run was Ben Nevis, who'd moved into the leading half dozen, still headed by Delmoss, Rough and Tumble, Kininvie, and Prince Rock.

"In spite of aid from the saddle, Prince Rock found the 19th, an open ditch, all too daunting and dug his toes in, bringing Kininvie down with him. Going towards Becher's for the second time, Charlie brought Ben Nevis past a couple more tiring rivals and in fact actually took off a half length in front. Here, Delmoss crumpled and suddenly the Baltimore banker found himself in front by six lengths. . . There was no stopping Charlie. Rough and Tumble and John Francome went in valiant pursuit, as did. . . The Pilgarlic, but, try as they did, they couldn't narrow the gap. Coming into the second last, John asked Rough and Tumble for one final effort but the tank was now dry and, as the crowd roared their salute, 20

Becher's Brook, second circuit. Ben Nevis is #6.

lengths separated Ben from his nearest rival up the grueling run-in."

"After the last fence I realized I was going to win, but I couldn't think about it much yet," says Charlie. "I remembered walking the course with Graham and him saying when we got to the stretch, 'Now Charlie, if you get here and there is nobody in front of you, don't let up. Keep your head down and keep riding. Don't let up!' At the time he said that, I thought, 'Please, just let me get to this place, never mind about not having anyone in front of me!' But in the race, when I got to that spot I remembered Graham's words and I kept saying to myself, 'Don't let up. Don't let up!'"

Ann, Jay Griswold, and Charlie's mother and stepfather watched the race together from the stands. While they were natu-

Charlie and Ben Nevis, still jumping easily at the end.

rally excited, their expectations were low at the start. There was no disappointment that Charlie was in the back of the field when he came around the first time; they hadn't anticipated anything different. The field was at the far end of the course, not visible to the crowd, when Ben Nevis got his first call from the announcer. Soon he was getting called often, and then they heard to their incredulous delight that he was in first place.

Griswold says, "We just couldn't believe our eyes when we saw Charlie out in front. It was amazing to go so quickly from the low subdued emotion to the incredible high. When he crossed the line, every one of us had tears streaming down our faces. We were laughing and hugging and crying. We just couldn't believe it."

Wearing Wallace Lanahan's smile, Charlie wins the race!

Charlie and Ben Nevis came into the finish still going strong. The 68,000 people packing the course and the stands cheered him home, 20 lengths ahead of Rough and Tumble. The Pilgarlic and Royal Stuart, in third and fourth place, respectively, were the only other finishers.

Charlie pulled up and walked around behind the stands to the unsaddling enclosure, surrounded by mounted policemen. Still, the crowd pressed close. Many people wanted to touch Ben Nevis, and Charlie remembers, "Everyone seemed as excited about it as I was and was hanging on the horse. There was an old guy who had his hands on the reins as though he were going to lead him in, and the guard had to get him off, and finally Paul got there. Ben knew he had won, and all of the confusion didn't seem to bother him."

Paul Simpson leading Ben Nevis to the enclosure.

Tim Forster had watched the race from the owners and trainers stand. "The thing I remember most distinctly is that when I saw Charlie was miles out in front on the second circuit, I thought I must be mad," he said. "I thought there must be other horses in front that I hadn't seen; I must have made a mistake. Then when I could see that he really was first, I saw that John Francome was behind him, and so then I thought what a pity, he's going to get

125

Horse and rider savoring the victory.

outridden on the run-in. But everything went in copybook fashion that second year.

"The other thing that stands out in my mind is that when Charlie got off, it was as if he had been for a 100-yard walk, and I thought to myself he must be the fittest man in the world."

Charlie recalls that when he got to the enclosure, "The first person I saw that I knew was Graham, and he was crying, but it all hadn't really settled in on me yet. I wasn't tired, either. Then Tim was there and Ann was there and my mother. Ann received the trophy for Mr. Stewart, and there was an interview right away which was televised. Then we went into a little room where Ann and I and Graham called Mr. Stewart."

Redmond and Ann Stewart were in Florida with their daughters, Nina Strawbridge and Kathy Ingalls and Kathy's husband

Ann accepting the trophy for her father.

David. Before the race, the wife of Forster's head lad at Letcome Basset had put in a call to them and then held her end of the telephone up to the television so that they could hear the broadcast. At first, Stewart had the phone but he kept asking Kathy if it was the right race and what was happening. Then he heard that Ben Nevis was out in front and became so excited he couldn't hear, and so he handed the phone over to Kathy.

She says, "I couldn't believe my ears! It seemed like such a long race, and I was shouting out what the announcer was saying and Daddy was shouting and everyone was all excited. Then when he won we were all cheering and somebody ran out for champagne. Then we began to get all of these telephone calls from overseas. It was all astonishing."

When Charlie and Ann telephoned, Stewart couldn't talk from the excitement. Ann began to cry again, and Graham was crying openly. He was so pleased that Charlie had won. He says that he felt so much a part of it all that he was as happy as when he had won it himself years before.

After the trophy presentation, it was time for them all to go to a press conference in a small room that was packed with reporters. After about 15 or 20 minutes of answering questions, they had had enough. Wallace Lanahan was outside the door waiting for them, and he was very excited. He couldn't say enough about how great it all was. Finally, they packed up the gear, and Ann and Johnny Shaw and Charlie carried it back to the car with a police escort.

Lanahan wished that there had been some police around earlier. "I had made an early bet on Ben when the odds were 40-1," he explained, "reckoning that the odds would come down and then I would lay off some of the bet. But when the books opened for the actual race, he was still 40-1, so I had all of it. I watched the race with my brother and we were so thrilled. We wanted to get to the winner's enclosure to congratulate Charlie, but there was this mass of humanity – 12, 14 people deep around him. It was absolutely fantastic. However, somewhere in all that crush, a pickpocket got to me and took my wallet with the ticket for my bet in it. I was terribly disappointed, but I went over to Ladbrooke's, with whom I had placed the bet.

"Fortunately, they were very well organized. They recognized the amount I had bet and the office where I had made the bet. I was very distraught that I had lost this ticket, which was for a bit of money, and they said, 'Don't worry, sa'. When do you want your money?' I said I'd like to have it right then, and they said they couldn't do that but if I went round to the office where I had placed the bet, they'd have the money for me on Monday morning. And they did."

Some friends quickly organized a party, telling everyone to meet at Cotswold Gateway in Burford. It was a long drive and on the way down, the events of the day began to sink in. "We had on the radio and heard it on the news," Charlie says. "Hearing it like that with some time to relax, all of a sudden I thought, 'My God, I won the race.'

"It really had not been an exhausting effort for Ben. One of the things I had feared was getting into an all-out stretch duel with a professional – that would have been bad and that didn't happen. John Francome, who was second, was probably as fine a jockey as there ever was, and I didn't need to get into a duel with him, that's for sure, so we were lucky to have been where we were."

Ironically, Francome had schooled Ben Nevis the week before over hurdles at Newbury. He had said to Forster afterward, "There is no way that horse can go four and a half miles – he pulls too hard."

Francome and another jockey, Andy Turnell, whose horse had fallen at the third fence, came to the party that night. The celebration must have had its difficult moments for them, but they were gentlemen and very generous about it all. Charlie was very appreciative of their graciousness.

About 40 people met at the restaurant, and it was predictably lively. At about 10:30 p.m., the race came on the news, and the whole party summarily left their dinners and rushed upstairs to watch. They crowded into a little room where a half dozen older people sat quietly; those folks didn't know what had happened, but it didn't take long to enlighten them, and pretty soon they were cheering and celebrating right along with the group.

"It was just so terrifically exciting," Johnny Shaw recalls. "Words can't describe it. You had goose bumps. It was such an emotional thing."

The celebration had no shadow on it because not one jockey or horse had been hurt.

The Fenwicks, Griswold, and Shaw spent the night at the Thorners' house, staying up most of the night talking and watching a video of the race over and over. Shaw says, "I remember Charlie watching the film and saying, 'Damn, I am such an amateur – I had my whip cocked.' Only Charlie would notice something like that at that point."

There was too much adrenaline flowing for anyone to sleep. It was light before they got to bed.

The next morning, after Charlie and Graham went for a ride with Charlie proudly sporting his Grand National quarter sheet, the media descended upon them. Charlie was on the radio and the television, and also gave several newspaper interviews. The papers had a field day with articles such as "Big Ben strikes at 40-1," "Yankee Doddle," "You're the Tops Ben Nevis," and "Charlie is the Yankee Dandy!"

In each interview, Charlie was quick to point out that he had been lucky and that he was just a passenger on the best horse that day. He described how it was such an honor to ride with the English jockeys. Finally, he said that the victory had much to do with the way he and the horse had been programmed by Tim Forster and Graham Thorner.

Wallace Lanahan tells of overhearing an English woman in his hotel say, after listening to an interview, "That young man is a great credit to his country."

There was another group of people who were ecstatic about the race: the residents of Fort Williams in Argyll, which stands in the shadow of the mountain, Ben Nevis. They won thousands of pounds, and there was literally dancing in the streets. In Glasgow, more than 100 customers of the Ben Nevis bar placed winning bets; the manager jubilantly reported that he had won 2,000 pounds. Additionally, there was the Irishman who placed a four-pound bet correctly picking the first three finishers. He won 70,000 pounds.

In the village of Letcombe Basset, there was general rejoicing as well. The villagers had come to know the Fenwicks and to take a personal interest in Ben Nevis. One local, Tommy Morgan, said, "Ben Nevis is our hero. We all had a bit on him, and he has done us proud." Coincidentally, Morgan, 74, had been Billy Barton's first English jockey 52 years earlier.

The morning after the race, Forster was awakened by a man on a ladder outside his window stringing up bunting to welcome home the victors. Someone hung a sign over Ben Nevis's stable door: "You may be small, but you're the greatest of them all." The Fenwicks arrived in time for Ben Nevis's triumphant homecoming, and the whole village turned out to give them an unrestrained and emotional greeting. In the excitement, the horse van driver forgot to pull on the hand brake when he got out to open the doors, and the van began to roll backward. He raced for the cab and jumped in and pulled on the brake. Catastrophe averted, good will and many beverages flowed freely as the village celebrated.

After a tearful but joyful goodbye the next day, the celebration continued when Charlie and Ann were toasted on the airplane going home. There was a big group to meet them at Dulles Airport outside Washington, D.C., and the press was there to record their return. It had been 18 months since they had first left for England with such high hopes.

Ben Nevis followed them a few weeks later and began his retirement. He and his old stablemate Dosdi lived out their lives together in the green fields of Western Run Valley on the Fenwicks' farm. Ben Nevis died in March 1995 but earned one further honor: In August 2009, he was inducted into the National Thoroughbred Racing Hall of Fame.

Final words for Ben Nevis must come from Charlie:

"He always tried. Never once did I feel that he did not try as best he could. He never shied, never refused a fence, never spooked at a certain kind of fence. He would have jumped the Rocky Mountains if I'd asked him."

*Ken Riley, proprietor of the local Butler Store and a great supporter
of the Fenwick/Stewart efforts, toasts the winners.*

Charlie on Dosdi, winning at the Elkridge Harford Meet
in 1980, one week after his win in England.

Afterword

It is true, certainly, that Ben Nevis was an extraordinary race horse. The Fenwicks are quick to point out their horse's natural abilities and to credit the many people who helped them achieve their goals for him. However, it was Charlie who, with Ann's constant backing, rode the horse and made the couple's dreams take shape. He got around the English Grand National course on a day when 26 other jockeys failed to do so; when, with one or two exceptions, luck played remarkably little part in the result. He had an iron determination and strength of will that carried him to victory.

The following are the words of Turney McKnight, who has known Charlie for most of their lives: "Charlie has a quality that has become more and more apparent as he has gained more confidence in his riding and has acquired more self-awareness. It is a mental toughness and discipline. I think there is almost nothing that Charlie relishes more than riding hard at the third to last fence at the Grand National here (in Maryland). I mean, riding as hard as he can on a bad jumper with another jockey alongside on a similarly bad jumper, because Charlie knows that his mental toughness is going to prevail, and it always does. He is able to get his horse over the fence while the other rider is saying, 'Oh God,' and then that rider and his horse are on the ground. With riders of equal ability on horses of equal talent, Charlie will win. It is a fearlessness and a determination – and an awareness of those qualities in himself – that does it.

"But it is not that Charlie takes shortcuts. I have ridden against a lot of riders, and only the very best are totally predictable in their fairness toward their fellow rider, and Charlie is that way. I don't think I ever in my whole riding career had to call out to Charlie during a race. He would never give you an inch you didn't deserve, but he would never take an inch away that was rightfully yours."

Charlie and Ann individually have continued to race, ride and train horses with great success. Both have trained multiple Hunt Cup winners since Ben Nevis. And the tradition of working with horses has gone on with the next generation of their families. Their son, Charles C. Fenwick III was a professional jockey for three years and then turned to timber racing. The timber races of note he has won include the 2008 Maryland Hunt Cup on Askim, trained by his mother. Nina Stewart Strawbridge's three children all have won timber races of note as jockeys, trainers, or both. Eldest daughter Kathy Neilson Mckenna trained Young Dubliner who won the 2002 Hunt Cup and set a new course record. Nina's other daughter Sanna Neilson Hendricks first rode to victory at the Hunt Cup in 1991 and her second win was in 1993 on Ivory Poacher, a horse trained by Ann Stewart and partly owned by her mother's first cousins, Redmond Conyngham Stewart Finney and Jervis Spencer Finney. Among the many winners she has trained is The Bruce, owned by her brother Redmond Stewart Strawbridge, and ridden to victory by him in the 2007 Hunt Cup.

*Charles C. Fenwick III after winning the Manor Race in
2009, with Charles C. Fenwick IV aboard.*

A final note:

It has been 30 years since Ben Nevis raced. Yet there are still stories to be told about him. Just a few weeks ago I heard a new one from Irv Naylor, owner and former jockey. He said that he was out hunting on the only day that Redmond Stewart ever tried to hunt Ben Nevis, which was also the only time Stewart ever got on his back. It first struck Naylor that Stewart was wearing black and white checked trousers, and second, that Stewart was not in control of his horse. In fact, Stewart, after wheeling around and stopping and starting, began to head away from the rest of the hunt. Someone called after him, "Hey, Redmond, where are you going with that horse?" And Irv heard him toss an answer over his shoulder as he was carried away from the field, "Anywhere he wants to go!"

Ben Nevis II: Races in America

1. March 9, 1975 Goshen Hunt Races
The Sandy Spring, for horses that have not started under rules in 1975, first division, about 1¼ miles, minimum, wt. 165. Purse: Trophy. Time: 2:18
  1. Ben Nevis
  2. Aristocrat (Labadie Mill Farm) Ross Pearce
  3. Sir Wonder (Tom Voss) T.H. Voss
Also ran: Brash Bid (Sal Cicero) Leigh Huntsman; What a Doc (Robin Kelly) owner; Southern Duke (Brandywine Stables) D.P. Ross, Jr.; Holmby Meadow (Gilmore Flautt III) Franklin Waters III; {Pulled up} Code Man (Charles Sherd) Jack Bisnett.

2. March 23, 1975 Middleburg Hunt Point-to-Point Races
The Louis Leith Cup (Perpetual), open timber race, about 3 miles, wt. 160-165. Time 6:23¹/₅
  1. Ben Nevis
  2. Lost Lamb (David V. Robinson) Skip Brittle
  3. Bent Page (Hunter Lott) Duncan Patterson
Also ran: Portobelo III (Bellavista Farm) Paddy Neilson; Fell Swoop (Halfway Farm) E. Marks; Gun Mount (Turney McKnight) owner; {Fell} Believe the Price (Mrs. Redmond Toerge) Jonathon Ruhsam.

3. March 27, 1976 Mr. Stewart's Cheshire Foxhounds Point-to-Point Races
The Cheshire Bowl open race, about 3 miles, 19 jumps, over fair hunting country, wt. 170 Purse: Trophy. Time 7:03
  1. Ben Nevis
  2. Danny's Brother (Brooklawyn Farms) Curt Crossman
  3. Mid Clare (Chris Collins) Bruce O. Davidson
Also ran: Devil's Brolly (Foxbrook Farm) R.P.S. Hannum; Oliphant (Mrs. Robert Neilds) Michael Plumb.

4. April 10, 1976 The John Rush Streett Memorial
For 4 yr olds and up who have never won 2 races in a recognized timber race, about 3 miles over natural country, wt. 155-165 Purse: Trophy. Time 6:13⁴/₅
  1. Ben Nevis
  2. Green Rd. (J. Fife Symington) J.B. Secor
Also ran: {Fell} Pat's Gamble (Mrs. H.L. Burkheimer) Warrington Gillett III; {Fell} Super Buper (Mrs. M. Gillian Fenwick) Thomas Voss; ({Lost Rider} Crazy Stripes (Stokes Lott) Bruce Fenwick.

5. April 17, 1976 The 11th Running of the Benjamin H. Murray Memorial

Steeplechase for 4-year-olds and up which have not won 2 races over timber at a recognized meeting, about 3 miles, wt. 152-176 Purse: $1,500. Time: 6:06

    1.Ben Nevis

    2.Stormin Norman (Mrs. John Schapiro) Warrington Gillet III

Also ran: {Fell} Semington (Wallace Lanahan) Paddy Neilson; {Fell} Durock (Stitler Vipond) owner.

6. May 8, 1976 Fair Hill Races

The Foxcatcher Hounds Steeplechase, timber steeplechase for 5-year-olds and up, about 3 miles over fair hunting country, wt. 157-170 Purse: $2,500. Time: 7:27²/₅

    1.Ben Nevis

    2.Jacko (Russell B. Jones, Jr.) Wendy Jones

    3.Devil's Brolly (Foxbrook Farm) Reese Howard, Jr.

Also ran: Gabby S (Christine Wetherill) Duncan Patterson; Idol Fellow (Helen Pollinger) Jonathon Ruhsam; Baudry (Rushmore Mariner) Ross Pearce.

7. April 2, 1977 Howard County Cup

Open timber race, wt. 165 Points awarded to rider for Governor's Cup Trophy. Time: 6:54

    1.Ben Nevis

    2.Coney Island (Jay Griswold) owner

Also ran:{Pulled up} Roman Blaze (Art Williams) owner.

8. April 23, 1977 The Grand National Point-to-Point

For the Grand National Point-to-Point Challenge Bowl in memory of H. Robertson Fenwick, about 3 miles, 4-year-olds allowed 5 lbs. Purse: $5,000. Time: 5:58⁴/₅. New Record

    1.Ben Nevis

    2.Pat's Gamble (Harry L. Burkheimer, Jr.) J.B. Secor

    3.Kinloch (Mrs. Eugene Weymouth) Paddy Neilson

Also ran: Perfect Cast (Audrey Riker) Turney McKnight; Burnmac (George T. Weymouth) R.P.S. Hannum.

9. April 30, 1977 The Maryland Hunt Cup
4 miles over 22 fences, 4-year-olds wt. 150; 5-year-olds wt. 160; older horses wt. 165. No half-bred or sex allowances or allowances for riders. Purse $6,000. Time: 8:48⁴/₅

    1.Ben Nevis
    2.Perfect Cast (Audrey Riker) Turney McKnight
    3.Moon Meeting (Foxharbor Stables) Ross Pearce

Also ran: Handsome Daddy (Fife Symington) Bruce Fenwick; {Pulled up} Essex II (Benjamin H. Griswold IV) owner; {Fell} Kinloch (George T. Weymouth) Paddy Neilson; {Fell} Koolabah (F. Samuel Wilcox III) Michael Plumb; {Fell} Count Turk (Melinda O. Rogers) Don Yovonovich; {Fell} Raford Boy (Foxbrook Farm) R.P.S. Hannum.

10. April 8, 1978 Elkridge-Harford Hunt Races
The S. Lurman Stewart Memorial Challenge Trophy, steeplechase about 3 miles, wt. 165

    1.Ben Nevis
    2.Still in All (Turney McKnight) owner

Also ran: {Pulled up} Green Road (Fife Symington) Bruce Fenwick.

11. April 22, 1978 The Grand National Point-to-Point
For the Grand National Point-to-Point Challenge Bowl in memory of H. Robertson Fenwick, about 3 miles, wt. 165, 4-year-olds allowed 5 lbs. Purse: $5,000

    1.Ben Nevis
    2.Still in All (Turney McKnight) owner
    3.Moon Meeting (Foxharbor) Ross Pearce

Also ran: Hammurabi III (Stanislaw Maliszewski) R.P.S. Hannum; Green Road (Fife Symington) Steve Secor.

12. April 29, 1978 The Maryland Hunt Cup
Four miles over 22 fences, 4-year-olds wt. 150; 5-year-olds wt. 160; older horses wt. 165. No half-bred or sex allowances or allowances for riders. Purse: $6,000 Time: 8:33³/₅. New Record

    1.Ben Nevis
    2.Perfect Cast (Audrey Riker) Turney McKnight
    3.Moon Meeting (Foxharbor) Ross Pearce

Also ran: Handsome Daddy (Fife Symington) Bruce Fenwick; {lost rider} Navy Davy (Mrs. Ernest Scott) Don Yovanovich.

References

Books
Gerry Cranham, Richard Pitman, with Joan Oaksey,
    The Guinness Guide to Steeplechasing
Dick Francis, *The Sport of Queens*
Gordon Grand, *Redmond Stewart, Foxhunter and Gentleman*
Elinor Stewart Heiser, *Days Gone By*
John Hughes and Peter Watson, *Long Live the National*
John Hughes and Peter Watson, Editors, *My Greatest Training Triumph*
Peter King, *The Grand National: Anybody's Race*
Jane McIlvaine, *The Will to Win*
John E. Rossell, *History of the Maryland Hunt Cup*
Dawn F. Thomas, *The Green Spring Valley*
Peter Winants, *Jay Trump*
Margaret Worrall, *100 Runnings of the Maryland Hunt Cup*
Margaret Worrall, *The History of the Green Spring Valley Hunt Club*

Magazines
The Blood Horse
The Chronicle of the Horse
Horse and Hound
The Maryland Horse

Newspapers
The Baltimore Sun
Daily Express
Daily Mail
The Daily Telegraph
News of the World
The Observer
The Sporting Life
The Sun
The Sunday Times
Sunday Mirror
Sunday People

Other
mybetting.com
National Hunt Annual
BBC Homepage

Breinigsville, PA USA
24 March 2010
234800BV00005B/2/P

9 780615 357416